NOT FOR SPECIALISTS

NOT FOR SPECIALISTS:
NEW AND SELECTED POEMS

W. D. SNODGRASS

AMERICAN POETS CONTINUUM SERIES, NO. 97

BOA EDITIONS, LTD. ✢ ROCHESTER, NY ✢ 2006

07 08 09 10 7 6 5 4 3 2

Publications by BOA Editions, Ltd.—a not-for-profit corporation under section 501 (c) (3)
of the United States Internal Revenue Code—are made possible with the assistance of
grants from the Literature Program of the New York State Council on the Arts;
the Literature Program of the National Endowment for the Arts; County of Monroe, NY;
the Lannan Foundation for support of the Lannan Translation Selection Series;
Sonia Raiziss Giop Charitable Foundation; Mary S. Mulligan Charitable Trust;
Rochester Area Community Foundation; Arts & Cultural Council for Greater Rochester;
Steeple-Jack Fund; Elizabeth F. Cheney Foundation; Eastman Kodak Company;
Chesonis Family Foundation; Ames-Amzalak Memorial Trust in memory of Henry Ames,
Semon Amzalak and Dan Amzalak; and contributions from many individuals nationwide.

See Colophon on page 252 for special individual acknowledgments.

Cover Design: Daphne Poulin-Stofer
Cover Art: "W. D. Under Arrest" by DeLoss McGraw, courtesy of the author and the
    artist
Interior Design and Composition: Richard Foerster
Manufacturing: McNaughton & Gunn, Lithographers
BOA Logo: Mirko

Library of Congress Cataloging-in-Publication Data

Snodgrass, W. D. (William De Witt), 1926–
    Not for specialists : new and selected poems / W.D. Snodgrass—1st ed.
        p. cm. — (American poets continuum series ; no. 97)
    ISBN 978–1–929918–77–5 (alk. paper) — ISBN 978–1–929918–76–8 (alk. paper)
    I. Title. II. Series: American poets continuum series ; v. 97.

PS3537.N32N68 2006
811'.54—dc22

2005054846

BOA Editions, Ltd.
Nora A. Jones, Executive Director/ Publisher
Thom Ward, Editor/ Production
Peter Conners, Editor/ Marketing
Glenn William, BOA Board Chair
A. Poulin, Jr., President & Founder (1938–1996)
260 East Avenue, Rochester, NY 14604

for Kathy
now and whenever

Contents

from *The Fuehrer Bunker*, 1977, 1995

from *Kinder Capers*, 1986–2004

from *Each in His Season*, 1993

New Poems

from
Heart's Needle
(1959)

These Trees Stand . . .

These trees stand very tall under the heavens.
While *they* stand, if I walk, all stars traverse
This steep celestial gulf their branches chart.
Though lovers stand at sixes and at sevens
While civilizations come down with the curse,
Snodgrass is walking through the universe.

I can't make any world go around *your* house.
But note this moon. Recall how the night nurse
Goes ward-rounds by the mild, reflective art
Of focusing her flashlight on her blouse.
Your name's safe conduct into love or verse;
Snodgrass is walking through the universe.

Your name's absurd, miraculous as sperm
And as decisive. If you can't coerce
One thing outside yourself, why you're the poet!
What irrefrangible atoms whirl, affirm
Their destiny and form Lucinda's skirts!
She can't make up your mind. Soon as you know it,
Your firmament grows touchable and firm.
If all this world runs battlefield or worse,
Come, let us wipe our glasses on our shirts:
Snodgrass is walking through the universe.

Ten Days Leave

He steps down from the dark train, blinking; stares
At trees like miracles. He will play games
With boys or sit up all night touching chairs.
Talking with friends, he can recall their names.

Noon burns against his eyelids, but he lies
Hunched in his blankets; he is half awake
But still lacks nerve to open up his eyes;
Supposing it were just his old mistake?

But no; it seems just like it seemed. His folks
Pursue their lives like toy trains on a track.
He can foresee each of his father's jokes
Like words in some old movie that's come back.

He is like days when you've gone some place new
To deal with certain strangers, though you never
Escape the sense in everything you do,
"We've done this all once. Have I been here, ever?"

But no; he thinks it must recall some old film, lit
By lives you want to touch; as if he'd slept
And must have dreamed this setting, peopled it,
And wakened out of it. But someone's kept

His dream asleep here like a small homestead
Preserved long past its time in memory
Of some great man who lived here and is dead.
They have restored his landscape faithfully:

The hills, the little houses, the costumes,
How real it seems! But he comes, wide awake,
A tourist whispering through the priceless rooms
Who must not touch things or his hand might break

Their sleep and black them out. He wonders when
He'll grow into his sleep so sound again.

Returned to Frisco, 1946

We shouldered like pigs along the rail to try
And catch that first gray outline of the shore
Of our first life. A plane hung in the sky
From which a girl's voice sang: ". . . you're home once more."

For that one moment, we were dulled and shaken
By fear. What could still catch us by surprise?
We had known all along we would be taken
By hawkers, known what authoritative lies

Would plan us as our old lives had been planned.
We had stood years, waiting, then, scrambled like rabbits
Up hostile beacheheads. Could we fear this land
Intent on luxuries and its old habits?

A seagull shrieked for garbage. The Bay Bridge,
Crawling with noontime traffic, rose ahead.
We'd have port liberty, the privilege
Of lingering over steak and white, soft bread

Offered by women, free to get drunk or fight,
Free, if we chose, to blow in our back pay
On smart girls or trinkets, free to prowl all night
Down streets giddy with lights, to sleep all day,

Pay our own way and make our own selections;
Free to choose just what they meant we should;
To turn back finally to our old affections,
Ties that had lasted so they must be good.

Off the port side, through haze, we could discern
Alcatraz, lavender with flowers. Barred,
The Golden Gate, fading away astern,
Stood like the latched gate of your own backyard.

April Inventory

The green catalpa tree has turned
All white; the cherry blooms once more.
In one whole year I haven't learned
A blessed thing they pay you for.
The blossoms snow down in my hair;
The trees and I will soon be bare.

The trees have more than I to spare.
The sleek, expensive girls I teach,
Younger and pinker every year,
Bloom gradually out of reach.
The pear tree lets its petals drop
Like dandruff on a tabletop.

The girls have grown so young by now
I have to nudge myself to stare.
This year they smile and mind me how
My teeth are falling with my hair.
In thirty years I may not get
Younger, shrewder, or out of debt.

The tenth time, just a year ago,
I made myself a little list
Of all the things I'd ought to know,
Then told my parents, analyst,
And everyone who's trusted me
I'd be substantial, presently.

I haven't read one book about
A book or memorized one plot.
Or found a mind I did not doubt.
I learned one date. And then forgot.
And one by one the solid scholars
Get the degrees, the jobs, the dollars.

And smile above their starchy collars.
I taught my classes Whitehead's notions;
One lovely girl, a song of Mahler's.
Lacking a source-book or promotions,
I showed one child the colors of
A luna moth and how to love.

I taught myself to name my name,
To bark back, loosen love and crying;
To ease my woman so she came,
To ease an old man who was dying.
I have not learned how often I
Can win, can love, but choose to die.

I have not learned there is a lie
Love shall be blonder, slimmer, younger;
That my equivocating eye
Loves only by my body's hunger;
That I have forces, true to feel,
Or that the lovely world is real.

While scholars speak authority
And wear their ulcers on their sleeves,
My eyes in spectacles shall see
These trees procure and spend their leaves.
There is a value underneath
The gold and silver in my teeth.

Though trees turn bare and girls turn wives,
We shall afford our costly seasons;
There is a gentleness survives
That will outspeak and has its reasons.
There is a loveliness exists,
Preserves us, not for specialists.

Heart's Needle

For Cynthia

*When Suibhne would not return to fine garments and good
food, to his houses and his people, Loingseachan told him, 'Your
father is dead.' 'I'm sorry to hear that,' said Suibhne. 'Your
mother is dead,' said the lad. 'Then all pity for me is gone from
the world,' said he. 'Your sister, too, is dead.' 'The mild sun
rests on every ditch,' he said, 'and a sister loves even though
unloved.' 'Your daughter is dead,' said the boy. 'And an only
daughter is the needle of the heart,' said Suibhne. 'And your
little boy, who sat on your knee and called you "Daddy"—he
is dead.' 'Aye,"said Suibhne, 'that is the drop that brings a
man to the ground.'"*

*He fell out of the yew tree; Loingseachan closed his arms
around him and placed him in manacles.*

—after The Middle-Irish Romance
The Madness of Suibhne

1

Child of my winter, born
When the new fallen soldiers froze
In Asia's steep ravines and fouled the snows,
When I was torn

By love I could not still,
By fear that silenced my cramped mind
To that cold war where, lost, I could not find
My peace in my will,

All those days we could keep
Your mind a landscape of new snow
Where the chilled tenant-farmer finds, below,
His fields asleep

In their smooth covering, white
As quilts to warm the resting bed
Of birth or pain, spotless as paper spread
For me to write,

And thinks: Here lies my land
Unmarked by agony, the lean foot
Of the weasel tracking, the thick trapper's boot;
And I have planned

My chances to restrain
The torments of demented summer or
Increase the deepening harvest here before
It snows again.

2

Late April and you are three; today
   We dug your garden in the yard.
 To curb the damage of your play,
Strange dogs at night and the moles tunneling,
   Four slender sticks of lath stand guard
      Uplifting their thin string.

 So you were the first to tramp it down.
    And after the earth was sifted close
 You brought your watering can to drown
All earth *and* us. But these mixed seeds are pressed
   With light loam in their steadfast rows.
      Child, we've done our best.

 Someone will have to weed and spread
    The young sprouts. Sprinkle them in the hour
 When shadow falls across their bed.
You should try to look at them every day
   Because when they come to full flower
      I will be away.

3

The child between them on the street
Comes to a puddle, lifts his feet
   And hangs on their hands. They start
At the live weight and lurch together,
Recoil to swing him through the weather,
   Stiffen and pull apart.

We read of cold war soldiers that
Never gained ground, gave none, but sat
   Tight in their chill trenches.
Pain seeps up from some cavity
Through the ranked teeth in sympathy;
   The whole jaw grinds and clenches

Till something somewhere has to give.
It's better the poor soldiers live
   In someone else's hands
Than drop where helpless powers fall
On crops and barns, on towns where all
   Will burn. And no man stands.

For good, they sever and divide
Their won and lost land. On each side
   Prisoners are returned
Excepting a few unknown names.
The peasant plods back and reclaims
   His fields that strangers burned

And nobody seems very pleased.
It's best. Still, what must not be seized
   Clenches the empty fist.
I tugged your hand, once, when I hated
Things less: a mere game dislocated
   The radius of your wrist.

Love's wishbone, child, although I've gone
As men must and let you be drawn
    Off to appease another,
It may help that a Chinese play
Or Solomon himself might say
    I am your real mother.

4

    No one can tell you why
the season will not wait;
    the night I told you I
must leave, you wept a fearful rate
    to stay up late.

    Now that it's turning Fall,
we go to take our walk
    among municipal
flowers, to steal one off its stalk,
    to try and talk.

    We huff like windy giants
scattering with our breath
    gray-headed dandelions;
Spring is the cold wind's aftermath.
    The poet saith.

    But the asters, too, are gray,
ghost-gray. Last night's cold
    is sending on their way
petunias and dwarf marigold,
    hunched sick and old.

Like nerves caught in a graph,
　the morning-glory vines
　　frost has erased by half
still scrawl across their rigid twines.
　　　Like broken lines

　　of verses I can't make.
　In its unraveling loom
　　we find a flower to take,
with some late buds that might still bloom,
　　　back to your room.

　　Night comes and the stiff dew.
　I'm told a friend's child cried
　　because a cricket, who
had minstreled every night outside
　　　her window, died.

5

Winter again and it is snowing;
Although you are still three,
You are already growing
Strange to me.

You chatter about new playmates, sing
Strange songs; you do not know
Hey ding-a-ding-a-ding
Or where I go

Or when I sang for bedtime, *Fox
Went out on a chilly night,*
Before I went for walks
And did not write;

You never mind the squalls and storms
That are renewed long since;
Outside, the thick snow swarms
Into my prints

And swirls out by warehouses, sealed,
Dark cowbarns, huddled, still,
Beyond to the blank field,
The fox's hill

Where he backtracks and sees the paw,
Gnawed off, he cannot feel;
Conceded to the jaw
Of toothed, blue steel.

6

    Easter has come around
  again; the river is rising
    over the thawed ground
  and the banksides. When you come you bring
    an egg dyed lavender.
  We shout along our bank to hear
our voices returning from the hills to meet us.
  We need the landscape to repeat us.

    You lived on this bank first.
  While nine months filled your term, we knew
    how your lungs, immersed
  in the womb, miraculously grew
    their useless folds till
  the fierce, cold air rushed in to fill
them out like bushes thick with leaves. You took your hour,
  caught breath, and cried with your full lung power.

Over the stagnant bight
we see the hungry bank swallow
    flaunting his free flight
still; we sink in mud to follow
    the killdeer from the grass
that hides her nest. That March there was
rain; the rivers rose; you could hear killdeers flying
    all night over the mudflats crying.

You bring back how the red-
winged blackbird shrieked, slapping frail wings,
    diving at my head—
I saw where her tough nest, cradled, swings
    in tall reeds that must sway
with the winds blowing every way.
If you recall much, you recall this place. You still
    live nearby—on the opposite hill.

After the sharp windstorm
of July Fourth, all that summer
    through the gentle, warm
afternoons, we heard great chain saws chirr
    like iron locusts. Crews
of roughneck boys swarmed to cut loose
branches wrenched in the shattering wind, to hack free
    all the torn limbs that could sap the tree.

In the debris lay
starlings, dead. Near the park's birdrun
    we surprised one day
a proud, tan-spatted, buff-brown pigeon.
    In my hands she flapped so
fearfully that I let her go.
Her keeper came. And we helped snarl her in a net.
    You bring things I'd as soon forget.

You raise into my head
a Fall night that I came once more
to sit on your bed;
sweat beads stood out on your arms and fore-
head and you wheezed for breath,
for help, like some child caught beneath
its comfortable wooly blankets, drowning there.
Your lungs caught and would not take the air.

Of all things, only we
have power to choose that we should die;
nothing else is free
in this world to refuse it. Yet I,
who say this, could not raise
myself from bed how many days
to the thieving world. Child, I have another wife,
another child. We try to choose our life.

7

Here in the scuffled dust
is our ground of play.
I lift you on your swing and must
shove you away,
see you return again,
drive you off again, then

stand quiet till you come.
You, though you climb
higher, farther from me, longer,
will fall back to me stronger.
Bad penny, pendulum,
you keep my constant time

to bob in blue July
   where fat goldfinches fly
over the glittering, fecund
   reach of our growing lands.
Once more now, this second,
   I hold you in my hands.

8

I thumped on you the best I could
   which was no use;
you would not tolerate your food
until the sweet, fresh milk was soured
   with lemon juice.

That puffed you up like a fine yeast.
   The first June in your yard
like some squat Nero at a feast
you sat and chewed on white, sweet clover.
   That is over.

When you were old enough to walk
   we went to feed
the rabbits in the park milkweed;
saw the paired monkeys, under lock,
   consume each other's salt.

Going home we watched the slow
stars follow us down Heaven's vault.
You said, let's catch one that comes low,
   pull off its skin
   and cook it for our dinner.

As absentee bread-winner,
I seldom got you such cuisine;
we ate in local restaurants
or bought what lunches we could pack
   in a brown sack

with stale, dry bread to toss for ducks
   on the green-scummed lagoons,
crackers for porcupine and fox,
life-savers for the footpad coons
      to scour and rinse,

snatch after in their muddy pail
   and stare into their paws.
When I moved next door to the jail
   I learned to fry
omelettes and griddlecakes so I

could set you supper at my table.
As I built back from helplessness,
   when I grew able,
the only possible answer was
   you had to come here less.

This Hallowe'en you come one week.
   You masquerade
   as a vermilion, sleek,
fat, crosseyed fox in the parade
or, where grim jackolanterns leer,

go with your bag from door to door
foraging for treats. How queer:
   when you take off your mask
my neighbors must forget and ask
   whose child you are.

Of course you lose your appetite,
  whine and won't touch your plate;
    as local law
I set your place on an orange crate
in your own room for days. At night

you lie asleep there on the bed
  and grate your jaw.
Assuredly your father's crimes
   are visited
on you. You visit me sometimes.

The time's up. Now our pumpkin sees
  me bringing your suitcase.
   He holds his grin;
the forehead shrivels, sinking in.
You break this year's first crust of snow

off the runningboard to eat.
  We manage, though for days
I crave sweets when you leave and know
they rot my teeth. Indeed our sweet
  foods leave us cavities.

9

  I get numb and go in
though the dry ground will not hold
  the few dry swirls of snow
and it must not be very cold.
A friend asks how you've been
  and I don't know

or see much right to ask.
Or what use it could be to know.
   In three months since you came
the leaves have fallen and the snow;
your pictures pinned above my desk
      seem much the same.

   Somehow I come to find
myself upstairs in the third floor
      museum's halls,
walking to kill my time once more
among the enduring and resigned
      stuffed animals,

   where, through a century's
caprice, displacement and
      known treachery between
its wars, they hear some old command
and in their peaceable kingdoms freeze
      to this still scene,

   Nature Morte. Here
by the door, its guardian,
      the patchwork dodo stands
where you and your stepsister ran
laughing and pointing. Here, last year,
      you pulled my hands

   and had your first, worst quarrel,
so toys were put up on your shelves.
   Here in the first glass cage
the little bobcats arch themselves,
still practicing their snarl
      of constant rage.

The bison, here, immense,
shoves at his calf, brow to brow,
 and looks it in the eye
to see what is it thinking now.
I forced you to obedience;
 I don't know why.

 Still the lean lioness
beyond them, on her jutting ledge
 of shale and desert shrub,
stands watching always at the edge,
stands hard and tanned and envious
 above her cub;

 with horns locked in tall heather,
two great Olympian Elk stand bound,
 fixed in their lasting hate
till hunger brings them both to ground.
Whom equal weakness binds together
 none shall separate.

 Yet separate in the ocean
of broken ice, the white bear reels
 beyond the leathery groups
of scattered, drab Arctic seals
arrested here in violent motion
 like Napoleon's troops.

 Our states have stood so long
At war, shaken with hate and dread,
 they are paralyzed at bay;
once we were out of reach, we said,
we would grow reasonable and strong.
 Some other day.

Like the cold men of Rome,
we have won costly fields to sow
   in salt, our only seed.
Nothing but injury will grow.
I write you only the bitter poems
      that you can't read.

   Onan who would not breed
a child to take his brother's bread
   and be his brother's birth,
rose up and left his lawful bed,
went out and spilled his seed
      in the cold earth.

   I stand by the unborn,
by putty-colored children curled
   in jars of alcohol,
that waken to no other world,
unchanging, where no eye shall mourn.
   I see the caul

   that wrapped a kitten, dead.
I see the branching, doubled throat
   of a two-headed foal;
I see the hydrocephalic goat;
here is the curled and swollen head,
      there, the burst skull;

   skin of a limbless calf;
a horse's foetus, mummified;
   mounted and joined forever,
the Siamese twin dogs that ride
belly to belly, half and half,
      that none shall sever.

I walk among the growths,
by gangrenous tissue, goiter, cysts,
    by fistulas and cancers,
where the malignancy man loathes
is held suspended and persists.
    And I don't know the answers.

The window's turning white.
The world moves like a diseased heart
    packed with ice and snow.
Three months now we have been apart
less than a mile. I cannot fight
    or let you go.

10

The vicious winter finally yields
    the green winter wheat;
the farmer, tired in the tired fields
    he dare not leave will eat.

Once more the runs come fresh; prevailing
    piglets, stout as jugs,
harry their old sow to the railing
    to ease her swollen dugs

and game colts trail the herded mares
    that circle the pasture courses;
our seasons bring us back once more
    like merry-go-round horses.

With crocus mouths, perennial hungers,
    into the park Spring comes;
we roast hot dogs on old coat hangers
    and feed the swan bread crumbs,

pay our respects to the peacocks, rabbits,
    and leathery Canada goose
who took, last Fall, our tame white habits
    and now will not turn loose.

In full regalia, the pheasant cocks
    march past their dubious hens;
the porcupine and the lean, red fox
    trot around bachelor pens

and the miniature painted train
    wails on its oval track:
you said, I'm going to Pennsylvania!
    and waved. And you've come back.

If I loved you, they said, I'd leave
    and find my own affairs.
Well, once again this April, we've
    come around to the bears;

punished and cared for, behind bars,
    the coons on bread and water
stretch thin black fingers after ours.
    And you are still my daughter.

from
After Experience
(1968)

"After Experience Taught Me . . ."

After experience taught me that all the ordinary
Surroundings of social life are futile and vain;

    I'm going to show you something very
    Ugly: someday, it might save your life.

Seeing that none of the things I feared contain
In themselves anything either good or bad

    What if you get caught without a knife;
    Nothing—even a loop of piano wire;

Excepting only in the effect they had
Upon my mind, I resolved to inquire

    Take the first two fingers of this hand;
    Fork them out—kind of a "V for Victory"—

Whether there might be something whose discovery
Would grant me supreme, unending happiness.

    And jam them into the eyes of your enemy.
    You have to do this hard. Very hard. Then press

No virtue can be thought to have priority
Over this endeavor to preserve one's being.

    Both fingers down around the cheekbone
    And setting your foot high into the chest

No man can desire to act rightly, to be blessed,
To live rightly, without simultaneously

You must call up every strength you own
And you can rip off the whole facial mask.

Wishing to be, to act, to live. He must ask
First, in other words, to actually exist.

And you, whiner, who wastes your time
Dawdling over the remorseless earth,
What evil, what unspeakable crime
Have you made your life worth?

The Examination

Under the thick beams of that swirly smoking light,
　　The black robes are clustering, huddled in together.
Hunching their shoulders, they spread short, broad sleeves like night-
　　Black grackles' wings; then they reach bone-yellow leather-

y fingers, each to each. And are prepared. Each turns
　　His single eye—or since one can't discern their eyes,
That reflective, single, moon-pale disc which burns
　　Over each brow—to watch this uncouth shape that lies

Strapped to their table. One probes with his ragged nails
　　The slate-sharp calf, explores the thigh and the lean thews
Of the groin. Others raise, red as piratic sails,
　　His wing, stretching, trying the pectoral sinews.

One runs his finger down the whet of that cruel
　　Golden beak, lifts back the horny lids from the eyes,
Peers down in one bright eye malign as a jewel,
　　And steps back suddenly. "He is anaesthetized?"

"He is. He is. Yes. Yes." The tallest of them, bent
　　Down by the head, rises: "This drug possesses powers
Sufficient to still all gods in this firmament.
　　This is Garuda who was fierce. He's yours for hours.

"We shall continue, please." Now, once again, he bends
　　To the skull, and its clamped tissues. Into the cran-
ial cavity, he plunges both of his hands
　　Like obstetric forceps and lifts out the great brain,

Holds it aloft, then gives it to the next who stands
　　Beside him. Each, in turn, accepts it, although loath,
Turns it this way, that way, feels it between his hands
　　Like a wasp's nest or some sickening outsized growth.

They must decide what thoughts each part of it must think;
    They tap at, then listen beside, each suspect lobe;
Next, with a crow's quill dipped into India ink,
    Mark on its surface, as if on a map or globe,

Those dangerous areas which need to be excised.
    They rinse it, then apply antiseptics to it;
Now silver saws appear which, inch by inch, slice
    Through its ancient folds and ridges, like thick suet.

It's rinsed, dried, and daubed with thick salves. The smoky saws
    Are scrubbed, resterilized, and polished till they gleam.
The brain is repacked in its case. Pinched in their claws,
    Glimmering needles stitch it up that leave no seam.

Meantime, one of them has set blinders to the eyes,
    Inserted light packing beneath each of the ears
And calked the nostrils in. One, with thin twine, ties
    The genitals off. With long wooden-handled shears,

Another chops pinions out of the scarlet wings.
    It's hoped that with disuse he will forget the sky
Or, at least, in time, learn, among other things,
    To fly no higher than his superiors fly.

Well; that's a beginning. The next time, they can split
    His tongue and teach him to talk correctly, can give
Him opinions on fine books and choose clothing fit
    For the integrated area where he'll live.

Their candidate may live to give them thanks one day.
    He will recover and may hope for such success
He might return to join their ranks. Bowing away,
    They nod, whispering, "One of ours; one of ours. Yes. Yes."

A Flat One

Old Fritz, on this rotating bed
For seven wasted months you lay
Unfit to move, shrunken, gray,
No good to yourself or anyone
But to be babied—changed and bathed and fed.
      At long last, that's all done.

Before each meal, twice every night,
We set pads on your bedsores, shut
Your catheter tube off, then brought
The second canvas-and-black-iron
Bedframe and clamped you in between them, tight,
      Scared, so we could turn

You over. We washed you, covered you,
Cut up each bite of meat you ate;
We watched your lean jaws masticate
As ravenously your useless food
As thieves at hard labor in their chains chew
      Or insects in the wood.

Such pious sacrifice to give
You all you could demand of pain:
Receive this haddock's body, slain
For you, old tyrant; take this blood
Of a tomato, shed that you might live.
      You had that costly food.

You seem to be all finished, so
We'll plug your old recalcitrant anus
And tie up your discouraged penis
In a great snow-white bow of gauze.
We wrap you, pin you, and cart you down below,
      Below, below, because

Your credit has finally run out.
On our steel table, trussed and carved,
You'll find this world's hardworking, starved
Teeth working in your precious skin.
The earth turns, in the end, by turn about
        And opens to take you in.

Seven months gone down the drain; thank God
That's through. Throw out the four-by-fours,
Swabsticks, the thick salve for bedsores,
Throw out the diaper pads and drug
Containers, pile the bedclothes in a wad,
        And rinse the cider jug

Half-filled with the last urine. Then
Empty out the cotton cans,
Autoclave the bowls and spit pans,
Unhook the pumps and all the red
Tubes—catheter, suction, oxygen;
        Next, wash the empty bed.

—All this Dark Age machinery
On which we had tormented you
To life. Last, we collect the few
Belongings: snapshots, some odd bills,
Your mail, and half a pack of Luckies we
        Won't light you after meals.

Old man, these seven months you've lain
Determined—not that you would live—
Just to not die. No one would give
You one chance you could ever wake
From that first night, much less go well again,
        Much less go home and make

Your living; how could you hope to find
A place for yourself in all creation?—
Pain was your only occupation.
And pain that should content and will
A man to give it up, nerved you to grind
        Your clenched teeth, breathing, till

Your skin broke down, your calves went flat
And your legs lost all sensation. Still,
You took enough morphine to kill
A strong man. Finally, nitrogen
Mustard: you could last two months after that;
        It would kill you then.

Even then you wouldn't quit.
Old soldier, yet you must have known
Inside the animal had grown
Sick of the world, made up its mind
To stop. Your mind ground on its separate
        Way, merciless and blind,

Into these last weeks when the breath
Would only come in fits and starts
That puffed out your sections like the parts
Of some enormous, damaged bug.
You waited, not for life, not for your death,
        Just for the deadening drug

That made your life seem bearable.
You still whispered you would not die.
Yet in the nights I heard you cry
Like a whipped child; in fierce old age
You whimpered, tears stood on your gun-metal
        Blue cheeks shaking with rage

And terror. So much pain would fill
Your room that when I left I'd pray
That if I came back the next day
I'd find you gone. You stayed for me—
Nailed to your own rapacious, stiff self-will.
        You've shook loose, finally.

They'd say this was a worthwhile job
Unless they tried it. It is mad
To throw our good lives after bad;
Waste time, drugs, and our minds, while strong
Men starve. How many young men did we rob
        To keep you hanging on?

I can't think we did you much good.
Well, when you died, none of us wept.
You killed for us, and so we kept
You, because we need to earn our pay.
No. We'd still have to help you try. We would
        Have killed for you today.

Lying Awake

This moth caught in the room tonight
Squirmed up, sniper-style, between
The rusty edges of the screen;
Then, long as the room stayed light,

Lay here, content, in some cornerhole.
Now that we've settled into bed
Though, he can't sleep. Overhead,
He hurls himself at the blank wall.

Each night hordes of these flutterers haunt
And climb my study windowpane;
Fired by reflection, their insane
Eyes gleam; they know what they want.

How do the petulant things survive?
Out in the fields they have a place
And proper work, furthering the race;
Why this blind fanatical drive

Indoors? Why rush at every spark,
Cigar, headlamp or railway warning
To knock off your wings and starve by morning?
And what could a moth fear in the dark

Compared with what you meet inside?
Still, he rams the fluorescent face
Of the clock, thinks that's another place
Of light and families, where he'll hide.

We'd ought to trap him in a jar,
Or come like the whitecoats with a net
And turn him out toward living. Yet
We don't; we take things as they are.

Lobsters in the Window

First, you think they are dead.
Then you are almost sure
One is beginning to stir.
Out of the crushed ice, slow
As the hands of a schoolroom clock,
He lifts his one great claw
And holds it over his head;
Now, he is trying to walk.

But like a rundown toy;
Like the backward crabs we boys
Splashed after in the creek,
Trapped in jars or a net,
And then took home to keep.
Overgrown, retarded, weak,
He is fumbling yet
From the deep chill of his sleep

As if, in a glacial thaw,
Some ancient thing might wake
Sore and cold and stiff
Struggling to raise one claw
Like a defiant fist;
Yet wavering, as if
Starting to swell and ache
With that thick peg in the wrist.

I should wave back, I guess.
But still in his permanent clench
He's fallen back with the mass
Heaped in their common trench
Who stir, but do not look out
Through the rainstreaming glass,
Hear what the newsboys shout,
Or see the raincoats pass.

What We Said

Stunned in that first estrangement,
We went through the turning woods
Where inflamed leaves sick as words
Spun, wondering what the change meant.

Half gone, our road led onwards
By barbed wire, past the ravine
Where a lost couch, snarled in vines,
Spilled its soiled, gray innards

Into a garbage mound.
We came, then, to a yard
Where tarpaper, bottles and charred
Boards lay on the trampled ground.

This had been someone's lawn.
And, closing up like a wound,
The cluttered hole in the ground
A life had been built upon.

In the high grass, cars had been.
On the leafless branches, rags
And condoms fluttered like the flags
Of new orders moving in.

We talked of the last war, when
Houses, cathedral towns, shacks—
Whole continents went into wreckage.
What fools could do that again?

Ruin on every side—
We would set our loves in order,
Surely, we told each other.
Surely. That's what we said.

Leaving the Motel

Outside, the last kids holler
Near the pool: they'll stay the night.
Pick up the towels; fold your collar
Out of sight.

Check: is the second bed
Unrumpled, as agreed?
Landlords have to think ahead
In case of need,

Too. Keep things straight: don't take
The matches, the wrong keyrings—
We've nowhere we could keep a keepsake—
Ashtrays, combs, things

That sooner or later others
Would accidentally find.
Check: take nothing of one another's
And leave behind

Your license number only,
Which they won't care to trace;
We've paid. Still, should such things get lonely,
Leave in their vase

An aspirin to preserve
Our lilacs, the wayside flowers
We've gathered and must leave to serve
A few more hours;

That's all. We can't tell when
We'll come back, can't press claims;
We would no doubt have other rooms then,
Or other names.

A Friend

I walk into your house, a friend.
Your kids swarm up my steep hillsides
Or swing in my branches. Your boy rides
Me for his horsie; we pretend
Some troll threatens our lady fair.
I swing him squealing through the air
And down. Just what could I defend?

I tuck them in, sometimes, at night.
That's one secret we never tell.
Giggling in their dark room, they yell
They love me. Their father, home tonight,
Sees your girl curled up on my knee
And tells her "git"—she's bothering me.
I nod; she'd better think he's right.

Once they're in bed, he calls you "dear."
The boobtube shows some hokum on
Adultery and loss; we yawn
Over a stale joke book and beer
Till it's your bedtime. I must leave.
I watch that squat toad pluck your sleeve.
As always, you stand shining near

Your window. I stand, Prince of Lies
Who's seen bliss; now I can drive back
Home past wreck and car lot, past shack,
Slum and steelmill reddening the skies,
Past drive-ins, the hot pits where our teens
Fingerfuck and that huge screen's
Images fill their vacant eyes.

No Use

No doubt this way is best.
No doubt in time I'd learn
To hate you like the rest
I once loved. Like an old
Shirt we unstitch and turn
Until it's all used out,
This too would turn cold.
    No doubt . . . no doubt . . .

And yet who'd dare think so
And yet dare think? We've been
Through all this; we should know
That man the gods have curst
Can ask and always win
Love, as castaways get
Whole seas to cure their thirst.
    And yet . . . and yet . . .

No use telling us love's
No use. Parched, cracked, the heart
Drains that love it loves
And still thirsts. We still care;
We're spared *that*. We're apart.
Tell me there's no excuse,
No sense to this despair. . . .
    No use . . . No use . . .

The Lovers Go Fly a Kite

What's up, today, with our lovers?
  Only bright tatters—a kite
That plunges and bobs where it hovers
  At no improbable height.

It's shuddery like a hooked fish
  Or a stallion. They reel in string
And sprint, compassing their wish:
  To keep in touch with the thing.

They tear up their shirts for a tail
  In hopes that might steady
It down. Wobbling, frail,
  They think it may now be ready

And balance their hawk aloft—
  Poor moth of twigs and tissue
That would spill if one chill wind coughed,
  Dive down to tear, or to kiss you;

Yet still tugs the line they keep
  Like some exquisite sting ray
Hauled from a poisonous deep
  To explore the bright coasts of day,

Or say it's their weather ear
  Keeping the heart's patrol of
A treacherous, washed-out year,
  Searching for one sprig of olive.

What air they breathe is wrung
  With twenty subtleties;
Sharp bones of failure hung
  In all the parkway trees;

It's enough to make you laugh—
  In these uncommitted regions
On an invisible staff
  To run up an allegiance!

Van Gogh: "The Starry Night"

Only the little
town
remains   beyond
all shock and dazzle
only this little
still
stands calm.

Row on row, the gray frame cottages, sheds
And small barns of an old Dutch town. Brownish-red
Houses with stepped gables and with high stoops,
With white or yellow doors. Plane over plane,
The angled roofs, receding, old as a memory
  what flowers were blossoming, how the fruit
  trees bore, had the nightingale been heard
  yet; the text of Father's sermon
Edge over edge, slate roofs ascending
Like the planes of a determined head,
Like stone stairs converging, step by step,
To its still dead-center, hurricane's eye,
This village chapel tiny as a child's toy
And as far.
  There is something about Father
  narrow-minded, icy-cold, like iron
                Face by face its quartz-blue
Salients upholding that slim spire into
The sky's rush, keen as your mother's needle
Pricking the horizon, mast firm in breaking
Waters, some lighthouse
  How could I possibly be in any way of any
  use to anyone? I am good for something!
                where there shines
No light.

Overhead: suns; stars; blind
                tracers bursting; pustules;
            swamp mouths of old violence
                                    Metaphysics
cannot hold   the dizzying heavens'
        shock   *chaos in a goblet*
            outspattering:
    eleven fixed stars; one sunburst
moon. Mid-sky, mid-spasm,
            the spiral galaxy
tumbling in trails of vapor like the high
        gods on Garganus
                        L'Art
            pour L'Art . . . L'Energie pour L'Energie
    when the holy ground burst
            into flower and a
        golden dew fell around, ethereal
first mists, thin
            dusts gathering into
        force and matter,
Chaos contains no glass
                of our caliber
            fusing
                destroying
        burning to be whole.

                Giotto and Cimabue live in an obeliscal
                society, solidly framed, architecturally
                constructed

Plane over plane, the village roofs in order,
Row on row, the dark walls of a town,
One by one, the ordered lives contained
Like climbers huddled to a rock ledge, pigs
Snuffling their trough, rooting at their dam.
    Every individual a stone and
    the stones clung together

Between the houses, fruit trees, or narrow
Lanes beneath the eaves-troughs and the dark
Shrubs; in back, laid out side by side,
The kitchen gardens with their heavy odors
Where dew sits chilly on the cabbage leaves
And a bird might sing
   And if no actual obelisk of too
   pyramidal a tragedy, no rain of frogs
Down those dark lanes you cannot see
A lantern moving or a shadow sway,
No dog howls, and your ear will never know
The footfall of some prowler, some lover's tread,
Some wanderer long gone,
  four great crises when I did not know what
  I said, what I wanted, even what I did.
              who cannot return.

the hollow dreams of revolutionaries . . .
they would wail in despair if once they
forgot the easy satisfaction of their
instincts, raising them to the unappeased
sufferings of the passions.

  Behind: blue mountains rising,
        range over range over range,
    Sometimes, just as waves break
       on sullen, hopeless cliffs
        earth's crust
    upthrusting its salt mass against
the sky; ton on broken ton of stone,
     the black earth hovering over,
       I feel a storm of
      desire to embrace something
    the ragged crests lumbering in,
  murderous as the seasons,
      bluer than the years,   *Painting*
  and much screwing are not

          compatible, man   relentless
     as a crowd pounds, blood
                    hammering the walls.
          becomes ambitious as soon as he
     becomes impotent.
          Its feathery surf,
                         first spies,
          already washing up around
     the gray outbuildings and the orchards
          to embrace something, a woman, a sort
               of domestic hen
          a spume of ancient
vacuum shuddering to reclaim
          its child;
                    so pale the
     groves of olives, gardens
          of agony, frothing about
     its feet in foam.

               In spring, a caged bird feels strongly
               there is something he should be doing.
               But what was it? He gets vague ideas.
               The children say, but he has everything
               he wants.

Down those dark streets which you can never see
     Shines just this much of light:
Eleven windows and one opened door—crystals
     Under tons of ore, clear garnets, warm;
Through those windows you can never see, and yet
     You always wonder who is waking there
Sitting up late over a pipe, sitting, holding
     Some pious, worn book between worn hands,
Who sits up late together talking, talking
     The night away, planning the garden for
Next year, the necessary furnitures,
     Who may be working, shredding the cabbages,

Darning some coarse fabric by a hanging lamp,
   Who may have gotten out of bed to calm
Their children fitfully sleeping, each
   In his own bed, one by one another,
Who goes to curry and bed down the patient beasts
   Warm in their old pens. But nothing moves
In those dark streets which you can never see,
   No one is walking or will ever walk there
Now, and you will never know

            Before: one black tree
                  between you and
      the town: one cypress mocks
            the thin blue spire, licking up
like flame—the green metabolism
                  of this forest sword
      that drives you from the town.
                  I have sown a little garden of poppies,
                  sweet peas and mignonette. Now we must
                  wait and see what comes of it.
Still, though, the little town, how peacefully
It lies under the watchful eyes of that
Fierce heaven.
   And the poor baby, too, whom I had
   cared for as if he were my own.
                  Nothing moves there yet, yet
How separate, how floating like a raft, like
Seaweed drifting outward on the tide, already
Dim, half gone,
   We take death to reach a star,
      diminishing into
Some middle distance of the past.
      some canvases that will retain their
      calm even in the catastrophe.

And still so calm
and still
so still

Zóó heen kan gaan.

from
Remains
(1970,1985)

The Mother

She stands in the dead center like a star;
They form around her like her satellites
Taking her energies, her heat, light
And massive attraction on their paths, however far.

Born of her own flesh; still, she feels them drawn
Into the outer cold by dark forces;
They are in love with suffering and perversion,
With the community of pain. Thinking them gone,

Out of her reach, she is consoled by evil
In neighbors, children, the world she cannot change,
That lightless universe where they range
Out of the comforts of her disapproval.

If evil did not exist, she would create it
To die in righteousness, her martyrdom
To that sweet dominion they have bolted from.
Then, at last, she can think that she is hated

And is content. Things can decay, break,
Spoil themselves; who cares? She'll gather the debris
With loving tenderness to give them; she
Will weave a labyrinth of waste, wreckage

And hocus-pocus; leave free no fault
Or cornerhole outside those lines of force
Where she and only she can thread a course.
All else in her grasp grows clogged and halts.

Till one by one, the areas of her brain
Switch off and she has filled all empty spaces;
Now she hallucinates in their right places
Their afterimages, reversed and faint.

And the drawn strands of love, spun in her mind,
Turn dark and cluttered, precariously hung
With the black shapes of her mates, her sapless young,
Where she moves by habit, hungering and blind.

The Mouse

I remember one evening—we were small—
Playing outdoors, we found a mouse,
A dusty little gray one, lying
By the side steps. Afraid he might be dead,
We carried him all around the house
On a piece of tinfoil, crying.

Ridiculous children; we could bawl
Our eyes out about nothing. Still,
How much violence had we seen?
They teach you—quick—you have to be well-bred
In all events. We can't all win.
Don't whine to get your will.

We live with some things, after all,
Bitterer than dying, cold as hate:
The old insatiable loves,
That vague desire that keeps watch overhead,
Polite, wakeful as a cat,
To tease us with our lives;

That pats at you, wants to see you crawl
Some, then picks you back alive;
That needs you just a little hurt.
The mind goes blank, then the eyes. Weak with dread,
In shock, the breath comes short;
We go about our lives.

And then the little animal
Plays out; the dulled heart year by year
Turns from its own needs, forgets its grief.
Asthmatic, timid, twenty-five, unwed—
The day we left you by your grave,
I wouldn't spare one tear.

Viewing the Body

Flowers like a gangster's funeral;
    Eyeshadow like a whore.
They all say isn't she beautiful.
    She, who never wore

Lipstick or such a dress,
    Never got taken out,
Was scarcely looked at, much less
    Wanted or talked about;

Who, gray as a mouse, crept
    The dark halls at her mother's
Or snuggled, soft, and slept
    Alone in the dim bedcovers.

Today at last she holds
    All eyes and a place of honor
Till the obscene red folds
    Of satin close down on her.

Disposal

The unworn long gown, meant for dances
She would have scarcely dared attend,
Is fobbed off on a friend—
Who can't help wondering if it's spoiled
But thinks, well, she can take her chances.

We roll her spoons up like old plans
Or failed securities, seal their case,
Then lay them back. One lace
Nightthing lies in the chest, unsoiled
By wear, untouched by human hands.

We don't dare burn those cancelled patterns
And markdowns that she actually wore,
Yet who do we know so poor
They'd take them? Spared all need, all passion,
Saved from loss, she lies boxed in satins

Like a pair of party shoes
That seemed to never find a taker;
We send back to its maker
A life somehow gone out of fashion
But still too good to use.

Fourth of July

The drifting smoke is gone, today,
From the mill chimneys; the laborers from the great
Iron foundries are on strike. They celebrate
Their Independence her own way.

She stopped a year ago today.
Firecrackers mark the occasion down the street;
I thumb through magazines and keep my seat.
What can anybody say?

In her room, nights, we lie awake
By racks of unworn party dresses, shoes,
Her bedside asthma pipe, the glasses whose
Correction no one else will take.

Stuffed dogs look at us from the shelf
When we sit down together at the table.
You put a face on things the best you're able
And keep your comments to yourself.

It is a hideous mistake.
My young wife, unforgivably alive,
Takes a deep breath and blows out twenty-five
Candles on her birthday cake.

It is agreed she'll get her wish.
The candles smell; smoke settles through the room
Like a cheap stage set for Juliet's tomb.
I leave my meal cold on the dish.

We take the children to the park
To watch the fireworks and the marching band.
For hours a drill team pivots at command.
For hours we sit in the dark

Hearing some politician fume;
Someone leads out a blonde schoolgirl to crown
Queen of this warcontract factory town;
Skyrockets and the last guns boom.

I keep my seat and wonder where,
Into what ingrown nation has she gone
Among a people silent and withdrawn;
I wonder in the stifling air

Of what deprived and smokefilled town
They brush together and do not feel lust,
Hope, rage, love; within what senseless dust
Is she at home to settle down;

Where do they know her, and the dead
Meet in a vacancy of shared disgrace,
Keep an old holiday of blame and place
Their tinsel wreathe on her dark head?

We tramp home through the sulfurous smoke
That is my father's world. Now we must
Enter my mother's house of lint and dust
She could not breathe; I wheeze and choke.

It is an evil, stupid joke:
My wife is pregnant; my sister's in her grave.
We live in the home of the free and of the brave.
No one would hear me, even if I spoke.

To a Child

We've taken the dog out for his walk
　　To the practice football field;
We sit on a dead branch, concealed
In the scraggly brush and trees
Beside the stale, old spring; we talk our talk
　　About the birds and the bees.

How strange we should come here.
In the thick, matted grass, ten feet away,
　　Some twenty years ago I lay
　　　　With my first girl. Half-dead
Or half-demented with my fear,
　　I left her there and fled.

Still, I guess we often choose
　　Odd spots: we used to go stone-dapping
On the riverbanks where lovers lay
Abandoned in each others' arms all day
　　By their beached, green canoes;
　　You asked why were they napping.

We've sat on cemetery
Stones to sing; found a toad
Run over on the graveyard road
That no one had seen fit to bury;
　　We've deciphered dark
Names carved in stone, names in the white birch bark.

We've waded up the creek
Over sharp stones and through deep
Slime, toward its source; caught a turtle
And carried the thing home to keep.
　　At best, he lived a week.
We said that ought to make the garden fertile.

We learned the animal orders' name-
 tags, posted in the park;
We fed the llamas, fawns and goats that roam
 The children's zoo, a sort of Ark
 For the newborn, hurt or tame,
  A home away from home.

We heard a bantie chick there that had wandered
  Into the wrong pen
  Peeping, peeping, scurrying
  After a huge indignant hen
   That fled. You said we'd bring
  Our feather duster to crawl under.

  And I mailed you long letters
  Though you were still too young to read;
 I sent you maple wings that fly,
Linden gliders and torqued ailanthus seeds,
 Pine cones crammed with flyers that flutter
  Like soft moths down the sky;

  Told you how Fall winds bear
 The tree seeds out, like airmailed letters,
To a distant ground so, when they come up later,
 They will find, possibly,
 Rain, sun and the soil they need
  Far from the parent tree.

  They threw my letters out.
 Said I had probably forgotten.
 Well, we have seen the glow of rotten
Wood, the glimmering being that consumes
  The flesh of a dead trout.
 We have walked through living rooms

And seen the way the dodder,
That pale white parasitic love-vine, thrives,
Coiling the zinnias in the ardor
Of its close embrace.
We have watched grown men abase
Themselves to their embittered wives

And we have seen an old sow that could smother
The sucklings in her stye,
That could devour her own farrow.
We have seen my sister in her narrow
Casket. Without love we die;
With love we kill each other.

You are afraid, now, of dying;
Sick with change and loss;
You think of your own self lying
Still in the ground while someone takes your room.
Today, you felt the small life toss
In your stepmother's womb.

I sit here by you in the summer's lull
Near the lost handkerchiefs of lovers
To tell you when your brother
Will be born; how, and why.
I tell you love is possible
We have to try.

from
Selected Poems
(1957–1987)

An Elm Tree

in memory of Albert Herrick

The winter birds have come;
One of them knows my name:
     Chick-a-dee-dee-dee-dee-dee.
Now, a whole pack of them

Skinning past like hoods;
Up in the maples, hidden,
     One shuffles his deck of wings
And deals me a word, a word;

Then, like a struck spark, gone.
Yet, there's my sentence again
     From an oak branch overhead;
Another one, farther on

Jeers me behind the barn
Where the old path turns
     Past the smoldering mound
Where years of rubbish burn,

And out beyond to the grove
Of pine trees, chill as the grave,
     Where the sun's light never falls
But needles, steady as grief,

Sift up, muffling and soft,
The lower limbs crack off,
     And you sink halfway to the knee
In what shone green, aloft,

What will seep down and in
Before it sees light again.
     You *could* stop, but the bird
Says your name, then

You come out into the whole
Light of day on the hill
     Where, on the high cleared brow
Strongly arching still

Stands that blighted elm,
Rawboned, overwhelmed,
     Stripped like the old mad king
Of this vegetable realm.

This was your great-uncle's tree
That he watered every day—
     30 buckets and the spring
Half a mile away.

The leaves gone and the bark.
As if a man stood, stark,
     Till all had fallen away
But the nerves' field thrown on the dark

Woods behind his back.
A small boy, you came to the shack
     Where he lived alone on his land;
You felt ashamed and sick

At the dark, heavy stain
On your thin wrist all day
    After he shook your hand.
May that not wash away.

Old Apple Trees

Like battered old millhands, they stand in the orchard—
Like drunk legionnaires, heaving themselves up,
Lurching to attention. Not one of them wobbles
The same way as another. Uniforms won't fit them—
All those cramps, humps, bulges. Here, a limb's gone;
There, rain and corruption have eaten the whole core.
They've all grown too tall, too thick, or too something.
Like men bent too long over desks, engines, benches,
Or bent under mailsacks, under loss.
They've seen too much history and bad weather, grown
Around rocks, into high winds, diseases, grown
Too long to be willful, too long to be changed.

Oh, I could replant, bulldoze the lot,
Get nursery stock, all the latest ornamentals,
Make the whole place look like a suburb,
Each limb sleek as a teeny bopper's—pink
To the very crotch—each trunk smoothed, ideal
As the fantasy life of an adman.
We might just own the Arboreal Muscle Beach:
Each tree disguised as its neighbor. Or each disguised
As if not its neighbor—each doing its own thing
Like executives' children.

                              At least I could prune,
At least I should trim the dead wood; fill holes
Where rain collects and decay starts. Well, I should;
I should. There's a red squirrel nests here someplace.
I live in the hope of hearing one saw-whet owl.
Then, too, they're right about Spring. Bees hum
Through these branches like lascivious intentions. The white
Petals drift down, sift across the ground; this air's so rich
No man should come here except on a working pass;

No man should leave here without going to confession.
All Fall, apples nearly crack the boughs;
They hang here red as candles in the
White oncoming snow.

Tonight we'll drive down to the bad part of town,
To the New Hungarian Bar or the Klub Polski,
To the Old Hellas where we'll eat the new spring lamb;
Drink good *mavrodaphne*, say, at the Laikon Bar,
Send drinks to the dancers, those meatcutters and laborers
Who move in their native dances, the archaic forms.
Maybe we'll still find our old crone selling chestnuts,
Whose toothless gums can spit out fifteen languages,
Who turns there late at night in the center of the floor,
Her ancient dry hips wheeling their slow, slow *tsamikos*;
We'll stomp under the tables, whistle, we'll all hiss
Till even the belly dancer leaves, disgraced.

We'll drive back, lushed and vacant, in the first dawn;
Out of the light gray mists may rise our flowering
Orchard, the rough trunks holding their formations
Like elders of Colonus, the old men of Thebes
Tossing their white hair, almost whispering,

> Soon, each one of us will be taken
> By dark powers under this ground
> That drove us here, that warped us.
> Not one of us got it his own way.
> Nothing like any one of us
> Will be seen again, forever.
> Each of us held some noble shape in mind.
> It seemed better that we kept alive.

A Phoebe's Nest

This green is the green of live moss;
This gray is the breast-feathers' down;
This tan, tough vine-roots;
This brown, dead needles of longleaf pine;

And this, this coppery fine filament
That glints like the light-weight wire
Boys wind off a motor core,
This is my own love's hair.

It's 7% and escrow;
It's Mary Jane and despair;
The ancient aunts say: headaches if
Birds build with your hair.

Near our hedgerow, in a nest snarled
Like a fright-wig, young hawks shriek;
Great red-tails sail our winds all day
While small birds peck at their heads.

But under our kitchen floorboards
Where live wires wind through the dark
Our crewcut phoebe plaited this nest
Like a jetset high pompadour.

Will the birds get dandruff?
Or pubic lice?
Will we go bald as an egg?

They'll knit a fine pucket
To warm up their brats;
You'll find out what'll ache.

This oriole's basket is woven white
Hair of our wolfhound, gone for years;
Our walls are rough plaster, laced with
The oxen's manes that worked this place.

Up under our roofpeak, birds slip
Through the roughcut cherry and beech;
Bare yards over the head of our bed
Strange bills squabble and screech.

It's starlings stuck down the chimney;
It's where did you go? Nowhere.
It's peckerholes in the siding
And why did you park there?
It's swallows barnstorming the garage.
Things get in your hair.

Sometimes you find the young birds
Gone; other times they're dead;
Ones that stay faithfulest to their nest
Just somehow never got fed. Yet

Nerve ends circuit a memory;
Phone calls lattice the night;
That phoebe shuttled our cellardoor
All day every day of her life.

Some say better not get involved;
Send Hallmark if you care;
Some say they've come a long way
And haven't got much to spare;
Some say they're gonna have some fun;
Too bad you don't dare;
Some say it just isn't fair;
It stretches but it well might tear;
Get nylon or get wash-and-wear;
They want their fair share.

Polish *ciocias*, toothless flirts
   Whose breasts dangle down to there,
Triple sea-hags say: headaches if
   Birds build with your hair.

Still, my lady's brushing-in sunlight
Near our silver maples where,
Like Christmas strings or bright beadwork
We loop loose strands of her hair.

Owls

Wait; the great horned owls
Calling from the wood's edge; listen.
There: the dark male, low
And booming, tremoring the whole valley.
There: the female, resolving, answering
High and clear, restoring silence.
The chilly woods draw in
Their breath, slow, waiting, and now both
Sound out together, close to harmony.

These are the year's worst nights.
Ice glazed on the top boughs,
Old snow deep on the ground,
Snow in the red-tailed hawks'
Nests they take for their own.
Nothing crosses the crusted ground.
No squirrels, no rabbits, the mice gone;
No crow has young yet they can steal.
These nights the iron air clangs
Like the gates of a cell block, blank
And black as the inside of your chest.

Now, the great owls take
The air, the male's calls take
Depth on and resonance, they take
A rough nest, take their mate
And, opening out long wings, take
Flight, unguided and apart, to caliper
The blind synapse their voices cross
Over the dead white fields,
The dead black woods, where they take
Soundings on nothing fast, take
Soundings on each other, each alone.

Mutability

It was all different; that, at least, seemed sure.
We still agreed—but only that she'd changed.
Some things that you still loved might still endure.

You woke in your own big, dove-tailed bed, secure
And warm—but the whole room felt rearranged.
It was all different; that, at least, seemed sure.

Her lamp stood four-square—like your furniture;
The air'd gone tinged, though, or the light deranged.
Some things that you still loved might still endure

Outside. Your fields stretched, a parched upland moor
Where shadows paired and split, where lean shapes ranged.
It was all different; that, at least, seemed sure.

And that, from here on in, you could count on fewer
Second chances. Some rules might be arranged;
Some things that you still loved might still endure,

Though some old friends would close, soon, for the pure
Joy of the kill—no prisoners exchanged.
It was all different; that, at least, seemed sure.

Maybe the injuries weren't past all cure.
No luck lasts; yours might not, too long, stay estranged;
Some things that you still loved might still endure.
It was all different; that, at least, seemed sure.

The Last Time

Three years ago, one last time, you forgot
Yourself and let your hand, all gentleness,
Move to my hair, then slip down to caress
My cheek, my neck. My breath failed me; I thought

It might all come back yet, believed you might
Turn back. You turned, then, once more to your own
Talk with that tall young man in whom you'd shown,
In front of all our friends, such clear delight

All afternoon. You recalled, then, the long
Love you had held for me was changed. You threw
Both arms around him, kissed him, and then you
Said you were ready and we went along.

A Valediction

Since his sharp sight has taught you
To think your own thoughts and to see
What cramped horizons my arms brought you,
    Turn then and go free.

Unlimited, your own
Forever. Let your vision be
In your own interests; you've outgrown
    All need for tyranny.

May his clear views save you
From those shrewd, undermining powers
That hold you close just to enslave you
    In some such love as ours.

May this new love leave you
Your own being; may your bright rebirth
Prove treacherous, change then and deceive you
    Never on this earth.

Now that you've seen how mindless
Our long ties were, I pray you never
Find, all your life through, such a blindness
    As we two shared together.

My dark design's exposed
Since his tongue opened up your eyelids;
May no one ever lip them closed
    So cunningly as I did.

A Locked House

As we drove back, crossing the hill,
The house still
Hidden in the trees, I always thought—
A fool's fear—that it might have caught
Fire, someone could have broken in.
As if things must have been
Too good here. Still, we always found
It locked tight, safe and sound.

I mentioned that, once, as a joke;
No doubt we spoke
Of the absurdity
To fear some dour god's jealousy
Of our good fortune. From the farm
Next door, our neighbors saw no harm
Came to the things we cared for here.
What did we have to fear?

Maybe I should have thought: all
Such things rot, fall—
Barns, houses, furniture.
We two are stronger than we were
Apart; we've grown
Together. Everything we own
Can burn; we know what counts—some such
Idea. We said as much.

We'd watched friends driven to betray;
Felt that love drained away
Some self they need.
We'd said love, like a growth, can feed
On hate we turn in and disguise;
We warned ourselves. That you might despise
Me—hate all we both loved best—
None of us ever guessed.

The house still stands, locked, as it stood
Untouched a good
Two years after you went.
Some things passed in the settlement;
Some things slipped away. Enough's left
That I come back sometimes. The theft
And vandalism were our own.
Maybe we should have known.

Old Jewelry

This Gypsy bodice of old coins
    From seven countries, woven fast
So that a silver braidwork joins
    The years and places their tribe passed;

This crown-shaped belt, cast in Souflí—
    Jeweled, enameling on silver-gilt—
A trothplight, then that surety
    On which a family would be built;

This Roman fibula, intact
    From the fourth century though bent;
This Berber fibula, once blacked
    With layers of thick tar to prevent

Theft but that, scoured and polished, shone
    As luminous as it ever was;
This lapis, Persian, the unfading stone
Gold-flecked and implicate with flaws;

Brass arm bands, rings, pins, bracelets, earrings—
Something from nearly every place
We'd been. Once more to see these dear things
Laid out for buyers in a locked showcase.

I'd known them, each one—weighed in hand,
    Rubbed, bargained, and then with my love,
Pinned each one on for her, to stand
In fickle times for emblems of

What lasts—just as they must have once
    For someone long dead. Love that dies
Can still be wrung out for quick funds;
    Someone, no doubt, would pay the price.

A Seashell

Say that inside this shell, some live
Thing hungered, trembled to survive,
Mated, died. Lift this to your ear
The way the young, on tape decks, hear
What to become, or on the phone,
The old evoke a dial tone
To what they had. Your blood will pound
Down those bare chambers, then resound
Your own ear's caverns as a ground

Bass swells, the depths of some salt tide
Still tuned to our salt blood. Outside,
The woods, nights, still ring back each word.
Our young owl, though, that always heard
My hoot, then veered down through the dark,
Our fox that barked back when we'd bark,
Won't answer, though. Small loss, now, when
Friends ask that I not call again.
Our pulse homed in on each other's, then.

Last night, I heard your voice—caught on
Streets we once taped in Isfahan;
Then, in a mosque near Joppa, blent
With hushed devotions and lament.
Now, put the shell back down, at rest
Near this brain coral, this wren's nest,
These photographs that will stand here
On their shelf in the silent, dear,
Locked, empty house another year.

Love Lamp

There's our candle, on the bedstand still
That served, warm nights, for lovelight
And the rays of its glass panels played
On our entangled legs and shoulders
Like some sailor's red and blue tattoos
Or as cathedral stained glass alters
Congregated flesh to things less
Carnal, tinged by its enfolding glow.

What could that frail lamp seem
To prowlers outside—the fox, say, the owl,
Or to some smaller creature, shrieking,
Pierced in the clutch of tooth and claw
That interrupted love's enactments?
Our glancing flashlight, though, showed
Only scattered grey fur, some broken
Feathers, bloodstained, on the lawn.

Scuttling back to bed, a little
Chilled from the wet grass, we scratched
A match restoring our small gleam
To see there, sinking in soft wax,
The wings and swimming dark limbs
Of that moth—still there, hardened
By the years like amber. While I remember
The scathing fire-points of his eyes.

from
The Fuehrer Bunker
(A Cycle of Poems in Progress, 1977
The Complete Cycle, 1995)

Even if we lose this war, we still win,
for our spirit will have penetrated our
enemies' hearts.
— Joseph Goebbels

Mother Teresa, asked when it was she
started her work for abandoned children, replied,
"On the day I discovered I had a
Hitler inside me."

Chorus: Old Lady Barkeep

(As defeat in World War II approached, Berliners revived a figure from Renaissance song and verse, Frau Wirtin, in satirical poems about their leaders.)

Old Lady Barkeep had a Folk
Who got their gun when Hitler spoke;
    He bellowed, "Germany, waken!
Rise up; if any foe rejects us,
We'll broil their liver for our breakfast
    And fry their balls like bacon!

"If they bite back, the bloody cunts,
We'll bang them on two fronts at once;
    You can't resist a God!"
Like ladykillers at a dance,
His troops advanced in goosestep prance
Through Austria, Czechoslovakia, France,
    Then found they'd shot their wad.

Easter in 1945
Was April Fools' Day. The one drive
They could maintain was to survive.
    Through caves and cellar holes,
Ditches and subway tunnels then
These irresistible Supermen
    Crept like ants or moles.

Dr. Joseph Goebbels
Minister for Propaganda

—1 April 1945, 0930 hours.

(From his house on the Wannsee, he watches a 1000-plane air raid over Berlin. He sings a folk song from the wars of the 1600s.)

Days, American bombing flights
Crush us to ash and brick dust; nights,
The British burn us down. Up there,
None of our own planes anywhere.
Revive, rise, you Powers of the Air—
It's Easter! Ha!—we haven't got a prayer!

Pray, children, pray;
Swedes are on their way.

So "Red Berlin" burns—turning red
Again. Those same streets piled with dead
Where we once cracked men's skulls to win
Their hearts and high offices. Once in,
We swore we'd never leave except
Feet first—one promise we *have* kept.
Maybe we should have warned them, though:
Let this earth tremble when we go!

Oxenstiern will march this way
Teaching children how to pray.

[*turns from window*]

First time I saw a bombed-out city—
Dresden—corrupted me with pity.

Some suffocated, others burned
Alive; for lack of air, some turned
Black and hard—their body fat ran
Out like goose grease in a pan.

Then he'll roast the fat, young pullets;
Melt church windows down for bullets.

I clumped down those long stacks of dead
Weeping, weeping. Back here, I said
I wanted the full power for putting
This whole nation on a war footing.
Now the foe's halfway through our gate
The Chief gives me the power. Too late.

Bet, kinder, bet.

So once more, the Chief's wrong proves out
Better than my right. I, no doubt,
Could have curbed slaughter, ruin, terror—
Just my old sentimental error.
Our role is to wipe out a twisted
Life that should never have existed.

Morgen komm der Schwed:

Each Ami bomb, each Russian shell
Helps us to wipe away this hell
Called Europe, Man's age-old, unjust
Network of lies, pandering, lust,
Deformity. This is to be
Young again—idealistic, free.

Morgen komm der Oxenstierna

Once, my newscasters would disguise
Each loss as a triumph. Those lies

Were mere truths *we* misunderstood:
There's no evil we can't find good.

Will der kinder beten lerne.

[turns back to the window]

Let it all fall in, burn and burst.
Blest be who dares act out his worst
Impulses, give way to the thirst
For blood and show this for the accursed
Inferno we took it for, right from the first.

Bet, kinder, bet;
Pray, children, pray.

Our Father who art in Nihil,
We thank Thee for this day of trial
And for the loss that teaches self-denial.
Amen.

Martin Bormann
Personal Secretary to the Fuehrer

—1 April 1945, 0930 hours. Easter!

*(At his desk, he writes his wife while calculating
his status in the Nazi hierarchy.)*

Dearest Beloved Momsy Girl,
    Our hour of destiny is born! The Reds have scraped up every
last Slav lout to hurl at us. More troops, more tanks, more armor
every day.

        I win; win; win. Not one phone call,
        One letter gets past to the Chief.
            My enemies drop off like leeches.

Upstairs, 1,000 American planes are bombing us this minute. Our
Luftwaffe, of course, is nowhere to be seen.

        So fat Goering don't dare show his face.
        Out at his estate with all his womenfolk,
            Fine wines, all that luxury.

    Oh Momsy, such times I miss you most. Send 50 pounds at
least of honey to the shelter. I'll see to dried vegetables myself.

        No way he could succeed the Chief now.
        If I could just find some proof he's back
            On drugs. Probably paracodeine.

    Our dear old "Onkle Heinrich"—Himmler himself—has lost
his command at Army Group Vistula in the East.

Knew it; knew he'd fuck that up when I
Got that post for him. And that butthead
Thanked me "for my kind help!"

Even if he's still got his SS troops, the concentration camps, his
Gestapo, this must make terrible trials for his wife and children.

Still my worst enemy. Still got
All Europe shitting pink. Good reason:
Ten million Jews and Slavs.

Are they planning to get captured by the Americans? The Chief
calls that treason; Himmler could be . . . Why don't you take his
wife some of your homemade jam?

Or any way to prove he was in on the July
Bombplot against the Chief. Or he could have
Peace feelers to the West: treason on treason!

Himmler's post has been handed to Heinrici—regular Army man;
never even joined the party. Speer, though, just got all his old
offices back again.

Himmler's laying low at his sanatorium. We'll
Keep an eye on Speer. Goebbels is no threat.
He means it: he'll kill himself.

In such times, our Leader needs real heroes. Like you and me, sweet
Momsy, stalwart Nazis that think only how we can save our people.

Got them by the gonads, every one of them.
Another heavy blast! Fucking good thing we're
Under 12 solid feet of concrete.

Us, with our innate love of light, being forced by the Jews to live
like creatures of the underworld — that just fills me with rage!

Thine Alone,
Martin

Albert Speer
Armaments Minister

—1 April 1945, 2230 hours.

(Speer had earlier been dismissed for admitting the war was lost. Reinstated on 31 March, he re-enters the steps from the garden into the bunker.)

So
I am
Reborn?
For Easter?
Hitler's builder
Once more. But not to
Build. To turn out armor,
To supply for a war we cannot win,
Equipment to destroy this world, not
Build another. We sit together, he and I,
Like little boys playing with toy train models
Of his new Linz and Munich, of his vast, new Berlin.

Does this make sense to get back in his good favor when
he is failing, when all our enemies are closing in on
every side, when his power will soon be gone?
It will be easier to denounce me as one of
those who helped him to burn down
their cities, those who helped
to kill their young men
building cloud
castles,
toys.

And
Every day
The real cities
Crash down. He
Swears to me he will
Not defend Berlin, which
Would be to destroy Berlin.
I swear I still have faith, which
Means I'll destroy anything he orders.
So then I tell his generals, the gauleiters, our
Factory managers to disobey his direct command
For total destruction, for a barren, uninhabitable land.
Lord, Lord, who ever said that you can't build on lies?

Reichsmarschall Hermann Goering

—1 April 1945.

*(Goering, a World War I ace, now head of the
Luftwaffe, is in disgrace for its failures. At his
Karinhall estate, he questions himself.)*

And why, Herr Reichsmarschall, is Italy
Just like schnitzle? *If they're beaten,*
Either one of them gets bigger.
Neither's kept too firm a figure.
Still, all this humble pie you've eaten
Lately stuffs YOU out quite prettily.

So then, Herr Goering, how can we
Tell you and Italy apart?
Italy always wins by losing;
Meanwhile, I, adroitely using
High skills and cunning, mastered the art
Of flat disgrace through victory.

You led our Flying Circus; how
Could our war ace become a clown?
Both pad out extended fronts;
Both make their living from slick stunts;
All the same, both get shot down.
But only one's called "Meier" now.

Pray, could an old, soft football be
Much like a man in deep disgrace?
They don't kick back; don't even dare
Look up — the British own the air!
So, stick a needle in someplace;
Pump yourself full of vacancy.

But answer one more question, which is:
Are politicians like whipped cream?
Both will inflate themselves with gas;
Also, they both puff up your ass
Till you're exposed like some bad dream
Where you've grown too big for your britches.

Herr President, can we tell apart
An artful statesman from an ass?
Fat chance! One spouts out high ideals;
One makes low rumblings after meals.
But that's the threat of leaking gas
That all men fear! *Right — that's a fart.*

Last, could you give one simple rule
To tell a medal from a turd?
Both of them come from those above you
Delivering their true opinion of you.
Right! Here's your new medal, conferred
For vast achievements: April Fool!

HEINRICH • HIMMLER
REICHSFUEHRER • SS
FORMER • COMMANDER
ARMY • GROUP • VISTULA

• 1 • APRIL • 1945 • 1100 • HOURS •

(Stripped of command, Himmler withdraws to his sanatorium at Hohenlychen where he tries to cast his horoscope. MM = 76.)

ASTRAL • SIGNS • SUGGEST • WE • MIGHT •
BE • IN • TROUBLE • DURING • APRIL • BUT
CONCUR • OUR • LUCK • WILL • TURN • ALL •
DANGER • WILL • BE • AVERTED • AT • THE •
ELEVENTH • HOUR • WE • WILL • BE • SAVED

FORTUNATELY • BY • A • SUDDEN • DEATH •
GOOD • GRIEF • I • DO • HOPE • BUT • IS • IT
HITLERS • DEATH • THE • SUN • IN   LIBRA
INDICATES • THE • FALL • OF • PRINCES •
JUPITER • URANUS • IN • SAGITTARIUS •

KEEPS • PROMISING • A • BREAKTHROUGH
LARGE • OPPORTUNITIES • FOR • GROWTH
MANY • NEW • CHANCES • FOR • CELEBRITY
NATURAL • TIMIDITY • CHANGING • INTO
OPEN • BOLDNESS • NATURAL • TIMIDITY

PERHAPS • THEY • DIDNT • REALLY • MEAN
QUITE • THAT • MEANTIME • MY • SIGN • OF
ROYAL • CHANCE • PROVES • I • AM • TO • BE
SUCCESSOR • TO • THE • CHIEF • FURTHER
THIS • SIGN • IS • WELL • ASPECTED • BY •

URANUS • CONJUNCT • JUPITER • WE • MAY
VERY • WELL • LOSE • THE   WAR • BUT • ILL
WIN • ASSUME • POWER • AFTER • ALL • IF •
YOU • CANT • PUT • YOUR • FAITH • IN • THE
ZODIAC • JUST • WHAT • CAN • YOU • TRUST

Adolf Hitler

—1 April 1945, 2330 hours.

*(In the bunker's deepest level, Hitler sits before
the wall map in his conference room.)*

Down: I got it all. Almost.

[takes situation reports]

Deserters! Traitors! Heidelberg and Danzig
Handed over practically undamaged.
Some half a million squirm out of our glory.

Say that I spoiled my appetite.
Brat fed sick on sugartits.

And Magdeburg? Bremen? Who could we send
Who'd make their lives worth less to them?
Our best troops, sacked up in the Ruhr—too gutless
To even get themselves killed.

"Casualties? But that is what
The young men are there for!"

In our camps,
You tramp them down in ditches like dead leaves;
Nights, they squirm up through the offal . . .
Speer would let these ditchworms spawn;
But yesterday I put Speer back in office.
Truly, you regret how kind you've been.

My mother's cake-and-candy boy!

[throws down a report]

Americans at their Easter mass. Sick,
Snivelling, Jew Jesus of these Christians!

> Always my own worst enemy. Always
> let them slip out of my grasp.

On every side, my mercies gathering against me.
My half-brother, Alois, my brother-in-arms,
Ernst Roehm, who dared rise up against me.
And both of them came back to betray me.

> With my mother, my own way. She
> Rammed it down the old man's throat.
> Her open grave mouth speaking:
> "This ground will have you, too."

Then, then we hacked them down like trash rats,
All who'd learned too little. Or too much.
In sewers, ditches, let them lay there to be seen.

> So shall I swallow all this ground
> Till we two shall be the one flesh.

Before my firing squads, men heiled my name.
The Old Man, Hindenburg, praised my
Gallantry. Out of ten million speakers
My voice scattering like the farmers' rain.

> The evils I do not desire,
> I do and I survive.
> What crime I choose is
> God's Law; my lie, truth.

My nerves rang one, one with the iron worlds;
I moved among the Old Powers, beyond
Evil, beyond time or consequence once more.

Too late. The Powers move on.
Since Stalingrad, this shuddering
I can't control. This left arm shaking
Pinned down by the right. Too late.

[takes up reports]

Deserters. Traitors. Crude populations rising.

[throws down the reports, goes to his desk]

April. In our bombed-out gardens, pale leaf buds,
That sickly green scum filming the trees again.
Through cracked concrete, green shoots shove up to the light.

[writes an order]

Well, we can provide them, still, an Easter Fools' gift,
Give them something to look up to: a wartime decoration—
More deserters to hang up on their streetlamps.
Traitors blossoming on every tree still standing.
Stalin: count on his appetite. The leavings—belts, bones,
Buckles—nothing sticks in *that* man's craw.

So; we must go out now. Suppose
We could still find a little chocolate cake?
A teensy bit of schlag, perhaps?

Albert Speer

—12 April 1945.

(Near Prenzlau on the Eastern front, Speer has just met with Heinrici and Gen. Reymann, Commandant of Berlin, to subvert Hitler's "scorched earth" directive.)

We
Saved
The bridges
Into Berlin today;
Two million people will
Have gas, coal, power, water,
Food; have some chance to survive.
General Reymann has orders, Heinrici's
And mine, to blow up only bridges with no
Gas mains, water pipes, electric cables. We have
Broken our oaths, defied our Fuehrer's direct orders.
We tear down the order of our lives, hoping to save lives.

What can his order to destroy these bridges mean, but that
he will defend Berlin, after promising he'd let it live?
So I obey his promise, but not his direct command.
I have saved these bridges, at the risk of
my own life—saved them not from the
Russians, but *for* the Russians.
Will they spare any more of
us than Hitler would?
Will they spare me
for opening our
gates to
them?

                                          Yet
                                     We have
                                  Saved these
                              Lives; that cannot
                          Be otherwise than good.
                       Have saved these Germans, not
                    From the Russian guns, only from
                 Their own beloved leaders. To whom
              They stay loyal. And would have me hanged
           For disobeying him even though it saved their lives.
        Surely the West must move in to save the city. Patton
     Is in position to attack; is he one to obey insane orders?

Whoever takes this city, I have shown that I can build, can
     rebuild; shown that I can save what's needed. So do
          I think that, having saved these bridges, I've saved
               my own position, even saved my own neck?
                    My staff and secretary, though, know
                         which papers must be burned
                              or sent to which friends
                                   once they're edited
                                        into our own
                                             codes.

Magda Goebbels

—15 April 1945.

(Goebbels' sister has offered to take the Goebbels'
six children to evade the Russians.)

Now Joseph's sister's offered us the chance
    To send the children somewhere farther West
Into the path of the Americans
    To let them live. It might be for the best

To send the children somewhere; farther West—
    They could surrender there. It stands to reason
To let them live; it might be for the best,
    Yet our Fuehrer would brand that as flat treason.

They could surrender. There: it stands to reason
    You ought to save the few souls dear to you,
Yet our Fuehrer would brand that as flat treason
    To all we've thought. To be upright and true,

You ought to save the few souls dear to you,
    Though their survival could no doubt bring shame
To all we've thought to be upright and true.
    Living with strangers, they'd still bear our name

Though their survival could no doubt bring shame,
    The way they'd live; they'd have to turn. Once there,
Living with strangers, they'd still bear our name
    With our past; that could be too much to bear.

The way they'd live, they'd have to turn, once there,
    Into the path of the Americans
With our past. *That* could be too much to bear,
    Though Joseph's sister's offered us the chance.

```
HEINRICH•HIMMLER
REICHSFUEHRER•SS
FORMER•COMMANDER
ARMY•GROUP•VISTULA

•15•APRIL•1945•
```

(A trainload of Lebensborn children, many stolen from families in the East or illegitimate children of SS men, has mistakenly gone to Army HQ at Zossen, 20 miles south of Berlin. MM=72.)

```
ARYAN•PURITY•A•STRAIN•OF•GOOD•
BLOOD•THATS•ALL•WE•ASK•YET•IT•
CARRIES•WITH•IT•SUCH•ENORMOUS•
DANGERS•WE•MUST•MAKE•SURE•OUR•
ENEMIES•DONT•GET•A•DROP•OF•IT•

FOR•ALL•NORDIC•BLOOD•OUR•FOES•
GET•WILL•GROW•UP•&•NEVER•LEARN
HUMANE•VALUES•WONT•DEVELOP•OUR
INTEREST•IN•CULTURE•BEAUTY•AND
JUSTICE•SUCH•BLOOD•MUST•NEVER•

KNOW•ITS•PAST•THIS•SHIPMENT•OF
LEBENSBORN•CHILDREN•OUT•OF•OUR
MATERNITY•HAVEN•IN•THE•TAUNUS•
NEVER•MUST•FALL•INTO•THE•HANDS
OF•THE•RUSSIANS•OR•THE•WESTERN

POWERS•WE•NEED•THEM•TO•FULFILL
QUOTAS•FOR•OUR•NEW•ARMIES•&•TO
REPLACE•ALL•THE•JEWS•GYPSIES•&
SLAVS•WEVE•HAD•TO•WEED•OUT•OF•
THE•HUMAN•GARDEN•THESE•ARE•NO•

UKRAINIANS•OR•KASHUBS•THEY•ARE
VALUABLE•BIG•BLOND•&•BLUE-EYED
WHEN•YOU•HELD•INSPECTION•THERE
YOU•ALWAYS•FOUND•THEM•FRESH•AS
ZINNIAS•IN•A•WELL-SELECTED•BED
```

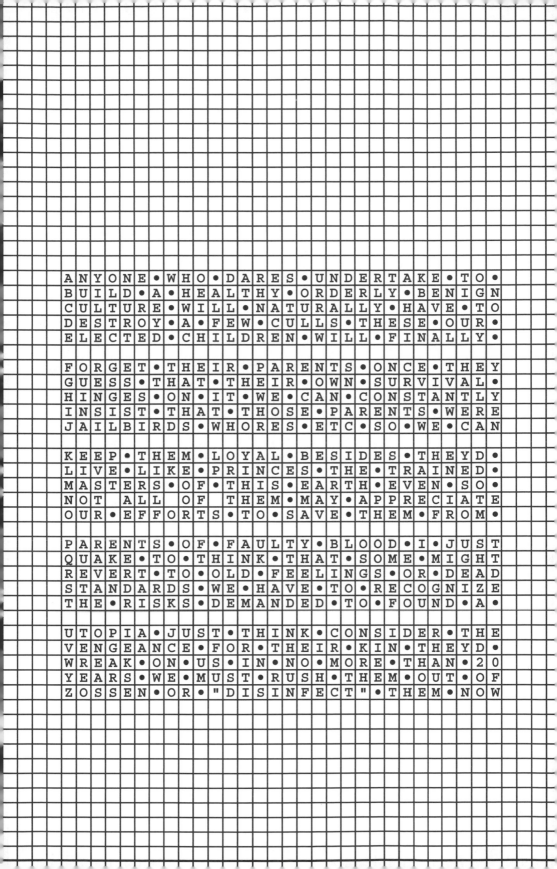

ANYONE • WHO • DARES • UNDERTAKE • TO •
BUILD • A • HEALTHY • ORDERLY • BENIGN
CULTURE • WILL • NATURALLY • HAVE • TO •
DESTROY • A • FEW • CULLS • THESE • OUR •
ELECTED • CHILDREN • WILL • FINALLY •

FORGET • THEIR • PARENTS • ONCE • THEY
GUESS • THAT • THEIR • OWN • SURVIVAL •
HINGES • ON • IT • WE • CAN • CONSTANTLY
INSIST • THAT • THOSE • PARENTS • WERE
JAILBIRDS • WHORES • ETC • SO • WE • CAN

KEEP • THEM • LOYAL • BESIDES • THEYD •
LIVE • LIKE • PRINCES • THE • TRAINED •
MASTERS • OF • THIS • EARTH • EVEN • SO •
NOT ALL OF THEM • MAY • APPRECIATE
OUR • EFFORTS • TO • SAVE • THEM • FROM •

PARENTS • OF • FAULTY • BLOOD • I • JUST
QUAKE • TO • THINK • THAT • SOME • MIGHT
REVERT • TO • OLD • FEELINGS • OR • DEAD
STANDARDS • WE • HAVE • TO • RECOGNIZE
THE • RISKS • DEMANDED • TO • FOUND • A •

UTOPIA • JUST • THINK • CONSIDER • THE
VENGEANCE • FOR • THEIR • KIN • THEYD •
WREAK • ON • US • IN • NO • MORE • THAN • 20
YEARS • WE • MUST • RUSH • THEM • OUT • OF
ZOSSEN • OR • "DISINFECT" • THEM • NOW

Adolf Hitler

—20 April 1945, 1900 hours.

*(After his birthday ceremony, Hitler withdraws
to his sitting room where he holds one of Blondi's
puppies. Earlier, he had gone up to the garden for
the last time.)*

Best stuffed in a bag and drowned.
This mockery: my best bitch
Pregnant once she can't survive.

The man will lie, supine; he, of course, will be completely naked.

My Effie's sister, Gretl, knocked up
By Fegelein. Luck lets me off just one
Humiliation: I breed no child.

His partner will assume her position, crouched over the head or
chest, as he prefers.

Pisspot generals wheedling for surrender,
For their cities, populations, lives.
Party maggots offering me presents;
Careful not to wish me a long life—
Their only shortcoming I fully share.

Only now may she remove her undergarments. Most frequently,
she will present her back to him.

Cub, in Landsberg Prison, my birthday flowers
Filled three prison rooms. The faithful
Sang beside me in my cell. I unwrapped
Presents, cut my cake. We had to laugh:
What?—was there no file inside it?

The cake my mother made me. . . . No. . . .

Exposed suddenly, the private parts can yield exquisite shock and pleasure.

> The Prison Governor's little daughter,
> Like this, curled up on my lap.

> > That's Edmund's cake, my brother's.
> > But I ate his. I spit on what was left.

She must not start at once; he must ask, must beg her, to begin.

> Oh, we hear their song:
> Live on. Live longer. Don't leave us
> To the Russian guns. Save us;
> Lead us to the mountains.

> > Oh stay! Don't leave us here forsaken.
> > Our men are waiting for their Leader.

> Back up again to Berchtesgaden?
> The locked elevator lurching up
> Through mountainsides of rock? Come out
> Over traitorous cities, lecherous faces,
> Jews with blond hair, blue eyes, who'd
> Steal our birthright, pull us down to slime.

He will grovel on the floor, declaring himself unworthy to touch her shoes, even to live.

> Two flights, today, to the garden. Schoolboys:
> Lined up like graves. Hands I have to touch.

It is not the mere fact of the excrement that matters.
Rather, he must be able to watch these emerge into existence.

Even the zoo beasts, my old neighbors, pacing
Till their keeper comes delivering
The right gift: one lead pellet.

She must now show disgust; may kick at him, revile him.

My pills; Morrell's injections.
My cake, chairs, rugs—without them,
Bare concrete. Same as any
Jew degenerate at Auschwitz.

Edmund died though, my brother,
When I was eleven. His birthday
Would have been eight days ago.

Only when he is fully excited by his own demands, may she yield
to his entreaties. The fear of taking these substances into his
mouth should heighten his excitement.

She'd lost three others. She, only
She, was glad I had survived.

Live on; only live. Don't
Leave us to the loneliness,
The spoiling of affections.

He kept me in. But she,
She made a special cake for me—

Over and over, I've said they could
Survive: overcome the facts.

Only the two of us together.

Now he should achieve his climax, alone and without assistance.

Our old Fighters—that was comradeship.
You have Blondi's underside. My diet cook,
My secretaries—they know how to listen.
Namesake, cub, you've done your month
In this filth. My cake; I'll eat it, too.

The Grail already calls its wanderer!

When he has washed and begged forgiveness, she may embrace
and comfort him.

My birthday present, my file: my
Cartridge of pure cyanide. Crawl back
Into the cave, work down in dry leaves . . .

Or she may lie down at his side.

An old dog deciding to lie down.

Eva Braun

—22 April 1945.

(Hitler's mistress received no public recognition and often felt badly neglected. Her small revenges included singing American songs, her favorite being "Tea for Two." Having chosen to die with him in the bunker, she appeared quite serene during the last days.)

Tea for two
And two for tea

      I ought to feel ashamed
Feeling such joy. Behaving like a spoiled child!
So fulfilled. This is a very serious matter.
All of them have come here to die. And they grieve.
I have come here to die. If this is dying,
Why else did I ever live?

Me for you
And you for me

     We ought to never flaunt our good luck
In the face of anyone less fortunate —
These live fools mourning already
For their own deaths: these dead fools
Who believe they can go on living...

And you for me
  Alone.

     Who out of all of them, officers, ministers,
These liars that despise me, these empty
Women that envy m—so they hate me—

Who else of them dares to disobey Him
As I dared? I have defied Him to His face
And He has honored me.

We will raise
A family

They sneer at me—at my worrying about
Frau Goebbels' children, that I make fairytales
For them, that we play at war. Is our war
More lost if I console these poor trapped rabbits?
These children He would not give me . . .

A boy for you
A girl for me

They sneer that I should bring
Fine furniture down this dank hole. Speer
Built this bed for me. Where I have slept
Beside our Chief. Who else should have it?
My furs, my best dress to my little sister—
They would sneer even at this; yet
What else can I give her?

Can't you see
How happy we would be?

Or to the baby
She will bear Fegelein? Lechering dolt!
Well, I have given her her wedding
As if it was my own. And she will have
My diamonds, my watch. The little things you
Count on, things that see you through your
Missing life, the life that stood you up.

Nobody near us
To see us or hear us

I have it all. They are all gone, the others—
The Valkyrie; and the old rich bitch Bechstein;
Geli above all. No, the screaming mobs above all.
They are all gone now. He has left them all.
No one but me and the love-struck secretaries—
Traudl, Daran—who gave up years ago.

> *No friends or relations*
> *On weekend vacations.*

That I, I above all, am chosen—even I
Must find that strange. I who was always
Disobedient, rebellious—smoked in the dining car,
Wore rouge when he said we mustn't.
When he ordered that poor Chancellor Schuschnigg
Was to starve, I sent in food.

We won't have it known, dear,
That we own a telephone, dear.

I who joined the Party, I who took Him
For my lover just to spite my old stiff father —
Den Alten Fritz! — and those stupid nuns.
I ran my teachers crazy, and my mother — I
Held out even when she stuck my head in water.
He shall have none but me.

> *Day will break*
> *And you will wake*

We cannot make it through another month;
We follow the battles now on a subway map.
Even if the Russians pulled back —
His hand trembles, the whole left side
Staggers. His marvelous eyes are failing.
We go out to the sunlight less each day. We live
Like flies sucked up in a sweeper bag.

And start to bake
  A sugar cake

He forbade me to leave Berchtesgaden,
Forbade me to come here. I tricked
My keepers, stole my own car, my driver Jung.
He tried to scold me; He was too
Proud of me. Today He ordered me to leave,
To go back to the mountain. I refused.
I have refused to save my own life and He,
In public, He kissed me on the mouth.

For me to take
For all the boys to see.

Once more I have won, won out over Him
Who spoke one word and whole populations vanished.
Until today, in public, we were good friends.
He is mine. No doubt
I did only what He wanted; no doubt
I should resent that. In the face
Of such fulfillment? In the face
Of so much joy?

Picture you
Upon my knee;
  Tea for two
And two for tea . . .

Dr. Joseph Goebbels

—22 April 1945.

*(On this date, Goebbels moved into the lowest
level of the bunker, taking a room opposite
Hitler's.)*

Stand back, make way, you mindless scum,
Squire Voland the Seducer's come—
Old Bock from Babelsberg whose tower
Falls silent now, whose shrunken power
For lies or lays comes hobbling home
Into this concrete catacomb.

Here's Runty Joe, the cunt collector
Who grew to greatness, first erector
Of myths and missions, fibs and fables,
Who pulled the wool then turned the tables:
He piped the tunes and called the dance
Where shirtless countries lost their pants.

Goatfooted Pan, the nation's gander
To whom Pan-Germans all played pander,
The jovial cob-swan quick to cover
Lida Baarova, his check-list lover:
Swellfoot the Tyrant, he could riddle
Men's minds away, hi-diddle-diddle.

Our little Doctor, Joe the Gimp,
Comes back to limpness and his limp:
Hephaistos, Vulcan, the lame smith
Whose net of lies caught one true myth:
His wife, the famous beauty, whored
By numbskull Mars, the dull warlord.

What if I took my little fling
At conquest, at adventuring,
Pried the lid of Pandora's box off—
There's nothing there to bring your rocks off.
I never saw one fucking day
So fine I courted it to stay.

If I got snarled in my own mesh
Of thighs and bellies, who wants flesh?
I never hankered after matter.
Let Hermann swell up, grosser, fatter,
Weighed down by medals, houses, clothing:
They leave me lean, secured in loathing.

As a young man, I pricked the bubble
Of every creed; I saw that rubble
And offered myself the realms of earth
Just to say Yes. But what's it worth?
No thank you, Ma'am. Behold the Ram
Of God: I doubt, therefore I am.

Here I forsake that long pricktease
Of histories, hopes, lusts, luxuries.
I come back to my first Ideal—
The vacancy that's always real.
I sniffed out all life's openings:
I loved only the holes in things.

So strip down one bare cell for this
Lay Brother of the last abyss.
To me, still, all abstractions smell.
My head and nose clear in this cell
Of concrete, this confession booth
Where liars face up to blank truth.

My tongue lashed millions to the knife:
Here, I'll hold hands with my soiled wife.
My lies piped men out, hot to slaughter;
Here, I'll read stories to my daughter
Then hack off all relations, choose
Only the Nothing you can't lose,

Send back this body, fixed in its
Infantile paralysis.
I was born small: I shall grow less
Till I burst into Nothingness,
That slot in time where only pure
Spirit extends, absent and sure.

I am that spirit that denies,
High Priest of Laymen, Prince of Lies.
Your house is founded on my rock:
Truth crows; now I deny my cock.
Jock of this walk, I turn down all,
Robbing my Peter to play Paul.

I give up all goods I possess
To build my faith on faithlessness.
Black Peter, I belie my Lord—
You've got to die to spread the Word.
Now the last act; there's no sequel.
Soon, once more, all things shall be equal.

Adolf Hitler

—30 April 1945, 1520 hours.

*(Russian troops are in Voss and Wilhelm Strasse.
Hitler and Eva have withdrawn to his sitting
room; she has already killed herself.)*

"To master the world and then
Destroy it."

More than fifty millions. More.
Who killed as much; who ever?

"Casualties? But that's exactly what
The young men are there for.
Casualties never can be high enough;
They are the seeds of future heroism."

Russian: twenty million.
Jew: seven million, five hundred thousand.

So many and what good? What does
That save you? It goes on, on, on . . .

Traitors on every side! Lies! Lies!

One gift, finally, to my faithful:
Last night, my secretaries, cook,
The short-wave girls—one capsule each
To save them from these Mongols'
Greasy pricks. A waste; some
Will sneak off West; some
Wait for the Red tanks . . . overcome
By their own lust . . .

Betrayed! Betrayed! Shamefully Betrayed!
Deceit! Deceit! Lying Past All Revenge!

Pole: three million.

And seven at one blow, one blow,
and seven at one blow.

Last night, again, the movie: Witzleben,
General Joke Life, handcuffed, wriggling
On the meat hook, hauled up naked,
Six times to strangle. Sir Choke Alive.
Five times hauled down, brought back,
Couldn't even beg to die. Scrawny pizzle
Couldn't come again. Not even dust.
Couldn't. . . .

Gypsy: four hundred . . . four . . .
four hundred thousand.

Shovelling lime in a latrine. Not one
Truly grateful. Oh, it's dragon seed.
We played it three times; no satisfaction.
Not even . . .

I bring you not peace but a sword.
This death in honor. This seed in the earth.

French: five hundred thousand.
Jugoslav: five hundred . . .

[turns to Eva's body]

Not even her who understood she died
For me and chose. Even to come here—
A mortal impudence.

> "The Grail Knight must never be suspected;
> Once recognized, then must he be gone."

Betrayed to! Lies! Betrayed to!

> German: spineless worms. Only four . . .
> four hundred . . . only four . . .

What use are facts, statistics?
To not need, ever, anyone alive. Whose
Death . . . whose death can show you
More fit to live? Whose . . .

> *Who's afraid of the big bad wolf,*
> *Ha-ha-ha-ha-ha!*

Tell me I have to die, then. You can't be
Sure enough. Relentless, every April,
My name on every calendar, my birthdate
Comes around. My Death is my own general,
My lickass lackey. My Will scrubs
You, all of you, all out . . .

"I go with the precision and
security of a sleepwalker."

> I pick my time, my place. I take
> This capsule tight between my teeth . . .
> Set this steel cold against my jaw . . .
> Clench, clench . . . and once more I am
> Winning,
>   winning,
>   winning . . .

Magda Goebbels

—30 April 1945.

(After Dr. Haase gave them shots of morphine,
Magda gave each child an ampule of potassium
cyanide in a spoon.)

This is the needle that we give
Soldiers and children when they live
Near the front, in primitive
    Conditions or real dangers;
This is the spoon we use to feed
Men trapped in trouble or in need,
When weakness or bad luck might lead
    Them to the hands of strangers.

This is the room where you can sleep
Your sleep out, curled up under deep
Protective layers that will keep
    You safe till all harm's past.
This is the bed where you can rest
In perfect silence, undistressed
By noise or nightmares, as my breast
    Once held you soft but fast.

This is the Doctor who has brought
Your needle with your special shot
To quiet you, so you won't get caught
    Off guard or unprepared.
I am your nurse who'll comfort you;
I nursed you, fed you till you grew
Too big to feed; now you're all through
    Fretting or feeling scared.

This is the glass tube that contains
Calm that will spread down through your veins
To free you finally from all pains
          Of going on in error.
This tiny pinprick sets the germ
Inside you that fills out its term
Till you can feel yourself grow firm
          Against all doubt, all terror.

Into this spoon I break the pill
That stiffens the unsteady will
And hardens you against the chill
          Voice of a world of lies.
This amber medicine implants
Steadfastness in your blood; this grants
Immunity from greed and chance,
          And from all compromise.

This is the serum that can cure
Weak hearts; these pure, clear drops insure
You'll face what comes and can endure
          The test; you'll never falter.
This is the potion that preserves
You in a faith that never swerves;
This sets the pattern of your nerves
          Too firm for you to alter.

I set this spoon between your tight
Teeth, as I gave you your first bite;
This satisfies your appetite
          For other nourishment.
Take this on your tongue; this do
Remembering your mother who
So loved her Leader she stayed true
          When all the others went,

When every friend proved false, in the
Delirium of treachery
On every hand, when even He
    Had turned His face aside.
He shut Himself in with His whore;
Then, though I screamed outside His door,
Said He'd not see me anymore.
    They both took cyanide.

Open wide, now, little bird;
I who sang you your first word
Soothe away every sound you've heard
    Except your Leader's voice.
Close your eyes, now; take your death.
Once we slapped you to take breath.
Vengeance is mine, the Lord God saith
    And cancels each last choice.

Once my first words marked out your mind;
Just as our Leader's phrases bind
All hearts to Him, building a blind
    Loyalty through the nation,
We shape you into a pure form.
Trapped, our best soldiers tricked the storm,
The Reds: though freezing, they felt warm
    Who stood fast to their station.

You needn't fear what your life meant;
You won't curse how your hours were spent;
You'll grow like your own monument
    To all things sure and good,
Fixed like a frieze in high relief
Of granite figures that our Chief
Accepts into His fixed belief,
    His true blood-brotherhood.

You'll never bite the hand that fed you,
Won't turn away from those that bred you,
Comforted your nights and led you
  Into the thought of virtue.
You won't be turned from your own bed;
Won't turn into the thing you dread;
No new betrayal lies ahead;
  Now no one else can hurt you.

Hermann Goering
Former Reichsmarschall

—1 May 1945.

*(Arrested by SS troops in his castle at
Mautendorf—left him by his mother's lover—he
stands naked before a full-length bedroom mirror.)*

When I speak to you, you stand to attention.
Straighten that back up. Lift up your damn head.
You'd featherbed your life out on some pension?
Fat chance of that, Fat Man! You're here to die.
You can't haul that much pork up in the sky
And if you go down and you fry instead
You'll spit like bacon. You lost your nerve
To face the life you once had; why not try
Making your exit with some style, some verve?

Disowned and disinherited? Poor baby!
We'll make a man of you, you slab of blubber.
We'll teach you where your toes are, your spine—maybe
Work you back down to fighting weight again.
Go turn in your silk robes, your diamonds, then
Give back all the paintings, cash in your rubber
Medals for the tub. From those big loose dugs
You'll get no warm milk. Join the world of men
Where pain and death live. And check in your drugs.

You might as well find out just what you've done,
Though that's not what they'll hang you for.
You took a fine officer's wife and son;
When you came to power you supplied
Facts that got your friend, Roehm, killed. Then you lied
About Blomberg and Fritsch. To start this war,

You threatened to bomb Prague; and your lies scared
Old Hacha till he gasped, fell, almost died.
Speak up to your Chief, though—you never dared.

No; one more time, you let yourself be mastered
By someone you sucked up to—who used your blind
Faith, used your worst impulses, then the bastard
Defiled your name. You bought your consequences.
Let Speer or Funk whimper and whine repentance
Merely to piss in front and crap behind
A few days more. You can't keep all *that* skin;
Keep some honor. You signed on for your sentence;
You're in so deep, there's no out left but in.

Your father lost the good name he'd once owned
By trying to fink out on his own past—
Your mother played the whore—and he'd condoned,
Ignored that for his soft life as a vassal
To Dr. Epenstein, lord of this castle—
Which he left you, where you end up at last
And you're about to end up. Own your own
Decisions; own your men. And if some asshole
Stands to face you down, you stand alone.

HEINRICH • HIMMLER
FORMER • REICHSFUEHRER • SS

• 1 • MAY • 1945 •

(Learning that Hitler's will names Doenitz as successor, Himmler ponders alternatives. MM=104.)

```
AN • EYE - PATCH • THATS • THE • ANSWER •
BESIDES • ILL • SHAVE • MY • MOUSTACHE
CUT • MY • HAIR • ALL • WRONG • THERE • MY
DISGUISE • IS • COMPLETE • ILL • WEAR •
EYEGLASSES • NOT • THIS • PINCE - NEZ •

FALL • INTO • THE • MOBS • OF • REFUGEES
GOING • WEST • IVE • BECOME • HEINRICH
HITZINGER • WITH • THE • LEGITIMATE •
IDENTITY • CARD • OF • A • SOLDIER • WE •
JUST • SHOT • AS • A • DESERTER • STILL •

KROSIG • SAYS • THE • ONLY • HONORABLE
LINE • IS • JUST • DRIVE • STRAIGHT • TO
MONTGOMERYS • H • Q • & • TELL • THEM • MY
NAME • IS • HEINRICH • HIMMLER • I • CAN
OFFER • MY • FORCES • SURRENDER • I • AM

PERSONALLY • RESPONSIBLE • WITHOUT
QUALIFICATION • FOR • ALL • S • S • ACTS
REALLY • NOW • WHY • NOT • JUST • SIMPLY
SHOOT • MYSELF • COULD • WE • GO • NORTH
TO • SCHLESWIG - HOLSTEIN • THEN • SET

UP • AN • S • S • GOVT • WE • MIGHT • OBTAIN
VERY • FAVORABLE • TERMS • FROM • THE •
WEST • SO • THEN • AT • THE • VERY • WORST
YOUD • KEEP • OUT • OF • THE • HANDS • OF •
ZHUKOV • AND • THE • RED • TROOPS • THE •
```

AMERICANS • OBVIOUSLY • THEY • WOULD
BE • BEST • BUT • WE • HAVE • NO • JEWS • WE
CAN • TRADE • NO • PRISONERS • WE • MUST
DO • WHAT • WE • CAN • TO • CONVINCE • OUR
ENEMIES • THESE • ARE • SUBSTANTIAL •

FORCES • BETTER • YET • WHY • CANT • WE •
GO • TO • FLENSBURG • WITH • DOENITZ • &
HIS • GANG • THAT • HITLERS • WILL • PUT
INTO • OFFICE • LINE • UP • OUR • CARS • &
JOIN • HIS • ENTOURAGE • WHOLL • DARE •

KEEP • US • OUT • BESIDES • NOW • THEYRE
LIKE • ANY • GOVT • THAT • WANTS • ARMED
MEN • TO • STAY • IN • POWER • SO • THEYLL
NEED • US • EVEN • TO • SURRENDER • ILL •
OFFER • MY • SERVICES • AND • DEMAND • A

POST • SAY • HEAD • OF • POLICE • WE • CAN
QUASH • THIS • SO-CALLED • LAST • WILL
REALLY • HES • NOT • BEEN • HIMSELF • MY
STARS • STILL • SAY • I • MUST • SUCCEED
THE • CHIEF • ALTHOUGH • ITS • HARD • TO

UNDERSTAND • HOW • THAT • CAN • BE • SO •
VERY • PUZZLING • STILL • FLENSBERGS
WHERE • YOUR • CHANCE • MAY • COME • OR •
YOU • CAN • ALWAYS • BITE • INTO • THIS •
ZINC • CAPSULE • & • WHAT • WHAT • WHAT •

Dr. Joseph Goebbels

—1 May 1945.

(Russian troops are within yards of the bunker.
After a brief ceremony, Goebbels and Magda
climbed to the garden and committed suicide.)

Say goodbye to the help, the ranks
Of Stalin-bait. Give too much thanks
To Naumann—Magda's lover: we
Thank him for *all* his loyalty.
Schwaegermann; Rach. After a while
Turn back to them with a sad smile:
We'll save them trouble—no one cares
Just now to haul us upstairs.

Turn away; check your manicure;
Pull on your gloves. Take time; make sure
The hat brim curves though the hat's straight.
Give her your arm. Let the fools wait;
They act like they've someplace to go.
Take the stairs, now. Self-control. Slow.
A slight limp; just enough to see,
Pass on, and infect history.

The rest is silence. Left like sperm
In a stranger's gut, waiting its term,
Each thought, each step lies; the roots spread.
They'll believe in us when we're dead.
When we took "Red Berlin" we found
We always worked best underground.
So; the vile body turns to spirit
That speaks soundlessly. They'll hear it.

Chorus: Old Lady Barkeep

Old Lady Barkeep squealed with laughter
When told she'd be forsaken after
    Her people's sorry loss.
She said, "There's always mobs to swallow
Lies that flatter them and follow
    Some savior to a cross.

"Don't kid yourself—I don't play modest;
As Greed and Cowardice's goddess,
    I thrive on just such ruin.
While humans prowl this globe of yours
I'll never lack for customers.
    By the way, how *you* doin'?"

from
Kinder Capers
(1986–2004)

Various works in collaboration
with the painter DeLoss McGraw

The Kinder Capers, 1986
A Colored Poem (The Locked House), 1986
The House the Poet Built, 1986
The Midnight Carnival, 1988
The Death of Cock Robin, 1989
To Shape a Song, 1989
Make-Believes: Verses and Visions, 2004

Seasoned Chairs for a Child

—from Make-Believes: Verses and Visions, *to accompany eight chairs, two for each season, made by DeLoss McGraw for the children's room of the Nashville, Tennessee, Public Library.*

Spring

Just when green leaves and bright songbirds arrive
A pert young god comes, too, decked out with wings
Plus bow and arrows. And though he shoots things,
They don't drop dead; they spring up more alive,
Strive, thrive, have kids—their kind just might survive.
And since he wears a blindfold, his bowstrings
Twang the same tune for beggars, bankers, kings:
"May your pulse thump, your juices jump and jive."

"I need Love like a black hole in my head,"
One young girl smirked. But just then Cupid's dart
Plinked by her ear. Through this small opening fled
All thoughts she'd need nobody. "Let's just start
Checking for someone with the right-shaped heart
To fill this gap," wholeheartedly she said.

Summer

Summertime comes and everyone takes wings,
But why catch planes when you could take a bird
And just land anyplace? So take my word:
Birds give the smoothest ride since old porch swings
Or merry-go-rounds with music and brass rings.
No seatbelts, please, and it would be absurd
To put on earphones—everybody's heard
That for your listening pleasure, a bird sings.

All girls fly Western style now—not side-saddle:
So pick a strong-winged mount with a tall crest
To skim across the prairies or skedaddle
Into a golden sunset in the West.
Then, when you're tired of galloping astraddle,
His wings and shoulders fold to form your nest.

Autumn

Now each leaf blazes like a candle flame
That, yellow, orange or red, catches your glance
While branches sway like arms in some fire dance
Before a sun god or a football game.
And yet if all this burning seems a shame,
Some bird lives in these woods, so there's a chance
He's like the phoenix that, as years advance,
Burns up like leaves, then gets reborn the same.

In due time, this year's leaves will fade and wilt,
Loosely scattering down in thick drifts, strewn
Like jigsaw pieces accidentally spilt.
Then through the gray oak trunks a Harvest Moon
Looks in to ask, "Have we all got our Crazy Quilt
Of warm leaves tucked in for the year?" Well, soon.

Winter

When winds have their big pillowfights, the air
Fills up with stormy feather-swarms that keep
Piling themselves outdoors into a heap
High as your eyebrow. You can't get anywhere;
Why not just curl up in our Winter Chair
And snuggle down into a long, warm sleep
Protected by the overstuffed, soft, deep
Arms of a comfy, star-marked Mother Bear?

What if you tried to go out for a stroll:
They'd stuff you into stiff snowsuits, socks, nubby
Sweaters, scarves, rubber boots 'til you'd look tubby
As any waddling, blubbed-up plump Bear Cub.
Your eyes keep oozing shut so why not roll
Back into your own dark, star-sparked cubbyhole?

W. D. Picks a Bouquet for Cock Robin But Cannot Separate the Thorns from the Flowers

—*from* The Death of Cock Robin

I found myself intent
To find profusions of rare bloom,
Harvesting armfuls that should scent
And ornament your room.

Or, failing that, some floral
Cordon summer might bequeath,
Or weave some ivy or live laurel's
Coronal and wreath.

Yet all my seasons' rambles,
Seeing I found nowhere to pick it
But in the flourishing, keen brambles
Of my brain's ingrown thicket,

Accept, then, this small vase
Of blossom, thistleflower and thorn
To lend some honor to the place
You rest, or to be worn.

W. D. Sits in Kafka's Chair and Is Interrogated Concerning the Assumed Death of Cock Robin

—*from* The Death of Cock Robin

Now "W"—we'll call you "W,"
    Okay? We like the friendly touch.
Just a few questions that won't trouble you
    For long; this won't hurt much.

First: name, age, sex, race, genus,
    Specific gravity and species;
Hat size, color of hair and penis;
    Texture and frequency of faeces?

Republican? No? Then a Baptist.
    If not, why not? If so, explain
Why you switched sides. Did your last pap test
    Turn pink or blue? Are you insane?

When did you halt, cease or desist
    Beating your wife? Was she friends
With this Cock Robin long? Please list
    Payments from foreign governments.

Have you changed sperm count or IQ
    Within six months? Signed a confession?
Why are we holding you? If you
    Don't know, then why ask you this question?

A simple yes or no is all
    We want; the truth always shines through.
Thank you. Please wait out in the hall
    Until somebody comes for you.

Auction

—from The Death of Cock Robin

For the gay tailfeathers, say, what'll you pay?—
Red, blue and purple plumes—a bouquet
Of heather-spume or a lit fountain's spray. Hey!
Shave a fine penpoint, whisk dust away
Or trim sharp the virginal's quills when you play.

Who'll buy an eye—aye, buy an eye!
This ringset onyx jet, black tack for your tie
Or oldtimer's photocell, spy in the sky,
Laserbeam click-ticking off who's slipped by
Or to glow soft by the cribside till dawntide draws nigh.

What am I bid for this swift wing?—
A deft wing, an arched-out lifting thing
To nail fast on your hallwalls or set fling
The soul's boomerang, the young shepherd's sling
That brings huge despair down, crowns the new king.

How much for the bones?—built-light-for-flight bones,
Leached, bleached-out, scaled to high kite zones—
Buoyance that scoured out, scored, then bored right, loans
Range to a flute floating out warm and bright tones
Over the vast frozen waste no man owns.

How far will you go for his hard, sharp toenails?—
For harp picks, guitar picks, to pick locks, open jails,
Thumb tacks, phononeedles, needles to sew sails,
To turn toward true North in high snowthrown trails
Or seek the soft South when winter winds blow gales.

For this heart, smart and artful, hey, where will you start?
A life's thump pump, formed to pyrite love's feverchart!
Let's throw in lights, liver, lungs, each left, torn apart,
Worn out part. Who'll start out—shebang and applecart
Go along; so what's wrong? Who'll buy a heart?

I, said the fly, I go for the eye.
Me, said the beetle, I'll buy me a bone.
Mine, said the earthworm, I take the heart.

The Capture of Mr. Sun

—*from* The Midnight Carnival

The sun is a lion
    circling his cage,
Caught for you, brought for you
    on this wheeled stage,
Through fixed bars glaring
    his wrath and his rage,
Like a pen for the baby
    or bedrails in old age.

The lion is a sunflower
    with a broad gold face,
Its petals outstreaming
    like a mane or the rays
Of that candescent Power
    we all watch pace
Through the gendering heavens
    on its circuit of days.

The flower is tracing
    the sun on its rounds;
The carnival moves through
    its orbit of towns;
The lion's cage rolls
    your streets up and down
where he pads and we shiver
    at his smile, his frown.

A Strolling Minstrel's Ballad of the Skulls and Flowers

—from The Midnight Carnival

Dahlia, Amaryllis, Iris,
    Flaunt their fragrance and their flair
As roman candles arc, desirous
    To burst new treasures on the air,
Spill out their color and their scent
    And whistle down the rambling bee.
When dazzle and pizzazz are spent
    And every garden's luxury
Of blossom's gone to shreds or hock,
    Where is that glamourie and that musk;
When January whips the stalk
    What memory stills the rattled husk?

By lurch and stumble, change and growth,
    Struggling from all fours, we rise
Cranking the backbone up, though loath,
    To lift our skull into the skies
Where the lit eye blinks out its longing,
    Gathers the world, then from that height
Sends hosts of bright ideas thronging
    Like fireflies sparking up the night.
What are that perfume and that pollen
    Or all the brain's fine fireworks worth
Once socket, stalk and spine have fallen
    As acrid, black ash drifts to earth?

The Carnival Girl Darkly Attracts W. D.

—*from* The Midnight Carnival

O she does teach the torches to burn bright
    As a rich jewel in an Ethiop's ear.
           Romeo,
           Romeo,
        Ro' me o-ver
        In the clo-ver
    Besides, what would I say to her?
Belle qui tient my vie
In this capture of your eyes.
      And would her mother let her out?
          And then? And then? And then?
Even as a common Italian young woman
Loaned her fresh visage to the holy mysteries,
So here, St. Anne, who's next to the Madonna,
    Donna?— that has to maybe be her name.
A glove, that I might touch that cheek.
        Ham and eggs
        Between your legs;
        Mine's got meat with gravy.
Je suis aymé by her whose beauty
Surpasseth all the wonders of the earth.
        She says she ain't nice
    And what she's doing here is working.
        Hath Dian's wit
And in strong proof of chastity well armed
        Two and two's four; five and four's nine.
    I can piss in yours; you can't piss in mine.
Beauty too rich for use, for earth too dear.
        They were only playing leapfrog
    So Nelly, keep your belly close to mine.

Wire Walker

—*from* The Midnight Carnival

This elevation's atmosphere's
Thin in your lungs, chill on your ears,

And the crowd's prayers, like hot air, rise
In hopes you'll fall before their eyes

Cracking your bones back to their level
Like wrecked kites or some downcast devil;

Soon as they've handed you their laurel,
Thorn or gold crown, there's a choral
Wail of dissent: "Are such heights moral?

Let's check his feet for the pure slime
We live in; some deep flaw or crime
Drives any anti-social-climb."

They'd have each high muckety-muck,
Poobah, or savior shit-out-of-luck
And shot down—a lame, ruptured duck—

So they applaud my heavy friend as
He steals the net from my stupendous
Finale: Last of The Wallendas.

They cheer the fall of every sparrow.
Mounting my bicycle or wheelbarrow,
I keep strict to the straight and narrow;

This road's shoulders are less than soft.
As waves of their ill feeling waft
Upwards, ill winds blow me aloft

Where, as hawks draft on thermal currents,
I bank on ill-will: flight insurance
Drawn on my uplift and endurance.

Ambling this bright, unfriendly skyway,
I can't roam one dark lane or byway;
Straight, straight ahead lies my way;
Who needs lane-lines are this lone highway?

The Drunken Minstrel Rags His Bluegrass Lute

—from The Midnight Carnival

I dreamed I heard all them people say,
"Get that thing out of here; take it away.

A man who plays when days are green
May sing absurd but not obscene

Blue movie music or some tune
You'd wail under a cold blue moon.

Twang us no twangs of ill-repute;
Mama don't 'llow no bluegrass lute."

        Bluegrass was all my joy to sang;
        Bluegrass was my delight—Gol dang!

        I'm too coarse to make common cause
        With blue stockings and their cool blue laws.

        My lute's sky-blue as a sky could be
        And shaded out toward infinity

        But I need dirt beneath my sky
        To plink it low and plunk it high.

They say, "Man winneth no awards
For words untimely, tunes untowards;

No fellowships and far fewer honors
For filthy facts and mixed up genres.

We like things simple, sweet and pure;
You play atonal, sing obscure,

Warble murder, deceit and sin;
Don't you care how square we been?"

      I built this lute of blue mahiou;
      That's why my quartertones turn blue.

      I strung its strings from pole to pole
      Over the belly and carved sound-hole,

      Then blew a bubble through my nose,
      A filmy globe of them and those,

      A world that, twirled upon its axis,
      Glitters with gritty facts and praxis.

They say, "Your song's unmentionable matter
Hurts our ears, makes our teeth chatter.

Go get your lute a coat of paint;
Jazz these things up the way they ain't.

Abstract us a whole kaleidoscope:
Red for passion, green for hope,

Purple ideas, a big pink song—
We got some rights and we ain't wrong!"

      But ha-ha, this-a-way it goes:
      The lily and the red, red rose,

      Oh, and the black bug on the ground.
      As moonshine lusters all around,

      I light on lovers, traitors, rich,
      Starved, what drops in the rank ditch,

      The blue hues of a world of men.
      It's ha-ha, this-a-way, then-oh-then!

They say, "Your songs do not compute.
Your music's mixed; your moral's moot;

Your chords are foreign. We should boot
You straight out of the institute

And hire some right-minded deafmute.
Go snuff that song back up your snout;

Just get that lowdown lute right out
And don't come back, you bluegrass lout.

       Whether I yodel, jive or jazz
       Blue gives my world the hue it has,

       So for my high-toned song, I smugly
       Smuggle in all things vile and ugly

       To serenade my village Venus.
       Nothing else can come between us.

       You all go toot your snooty flute;
       My country chords stand resolute.

       Discord and dat makes a bluegrass lute.
       I jams true blue and dat's da trut'.

W. D. Studies the Spectra of Departure

—from To Shape a Song

In the perspective of the heart,
Those dearly loved, when they depart,
Take so much of us when they go
That, like no thing on earth, they grow
Larger when fleeing from the eye
Till they invest the vacant sky
With their dear presence, an existence
Lost in love's exponential distance:
They're our astronomy, our science
And starry myth; they are red giants.
As for ourselves who have been left
Behind, we find we've been bereft
Of our best being, of the whole
Mass that could matter to the soul;
This sort of thing can leave you blue.
And whether our pale, bloodless hue
Arises from the Arctic chill
Of energies that flared out—will,
Warmth and acetylene desires—
Or from excess of passion, fires
Turned in, we seem an endomorph
Of shrunken hopes; we're our white dwarf.
By loss of qualities, we are
Changed into a neutron star
Or part-time partner, off and on;
Worse still, we may recount what's gone
Until, self-justified by grief,
We're turned a sum-and-substance thief,
Drain and devour what dares come near,
Emptying all things we hold dear,
Till we collapse inside at last,
Taking all we've drawn with us, past
Recall, recovery or control,
Down our own depths as a black hole.

Disguised as Humpty-Dumpty,
W. D. Practices Tumbling

—from The Kinder Capers

What is more odious than all
Fencesitting, straddling a wall?
Why should we back away and stall
    Teetering here all day afraid of
    Showing the world the stuff we're made of?

We know a man by what he'll tumble
To; pride goes before a stumble.
It's falling keeps a body humble.
    Some fall to work, some to their meal;
    All life must fall with Fortune's wheel.

Some use their training and their talents
To walk up wires and keep their balance;
Some leap, all buoyancy and valiance,
    In broad air; still we judge their worth
    When they've come back in touch with earth.

Into the nest of twig and feather
The egg must fall; the question's whether
You bounce back keeping things together.
    Some fall to tumbling in the hay;
    Some fall in love and crack that way.

Let others practice wings and Springs;
The falling leaf, the fall of kings
Ring out the old—the downward swing
    Of clocks and stocks, the Fall of Man,
    Fall is where everything began.

We hope to build this to a smash
Hit sport just like the Fender Bash,
The Fall from Grace, the Market Crash.
   The real point isn't winning; what's
   Important is to show some guts.

Dance Suite: Hip Hop

Lined up
Girls and boys,
Coins in the drop slot; wind-up toys;
Necks that switch
Every which way;
Join the Hip Hop, rapping like a robot.

Streets full of busfumes; stairs full of shovin';
TV's full of promises: luxuries and lovin';
Oil's on the water; spray's on the pumpkin;
Aspirin's full of strychnine, cyanide or somethin'.

Wig-wag
Knee joints,
Elbows crimped to zig-zag points;
Wrists and ankles
Twisted into angles;
Splayed-out fingers clamping into fists.

Sidewalks full of garbage; pictures in the news;
Mayor's on the radio spouting out excuses;
Bars on the storefronts; landlord's on the way;
Cops have got their Spring list—they'll make it pay.

Nuts and bolts
Charged by volts
Jumpstart into spastic jerks and jolts;
Gears and notches
Grinding crotches,
Juicing up the parts of the fools that watch us.

Ground's full of chemicals; ocean's full of waste;
Brother's full of steroids; meat got no taste;
Ceilings full of roaches; rats around the cradle;
Everybody's learned to read the lies on the label.

> Swirl around,
> Clown, on the ground,
> Twirling like a dervish whirls, upside down;
> Legs there,
> Kicking in the air,
> Striking like scorpions or Medusa hair.

A bullet's in the chamber; needle's in the vein;
Leg's set in plaster; no time for pain;
Street's full of dealers; girls are on the curbs;
Make a killing fast and get out for the suburbs.

> Shift your shoulder
> Like a soldier
> Ant, an identical mannekin or clone;
> Who can hurt a tall doll
> Rigid and mechanical
> Dancing the dictates of a microphone?

The Poet Ridiculed by Hysterical Academics

Is it, then, your opinion
        Women are putty in your hands?
Is this the face to launch upon
        A thousand one night stands?

First, please, would you be so kind
        As to define your contribution
To modern verse, the Western mind,
        And human institutions?

Where, where is the long, flowing hair,
        The velvet suit, the broad bow tie;
Where is the other-worldly air,
        Where the abstracted eye?

Describe the influence on your verse
        Of Oscar Mudwarp's mighty line,
The theories of Susan Schmerch
        Or the spondee's decline.

You've labored to present us with
        This mouse-sized volume; shall this equal
The epic glories of Joe Smith?
        He's just brought out a sequel.

Where are the beard, the bongo drums,
        Tattered T-shirt and grubby sandals,
As who, released from Iowa, comes
        To tell of wondrous scandals?

Have you subversive, out of date,
        Or controversial ideas?
And can you really pull your weight
        Among such minds as these?

Ah, what avails the tenure race,
Ah, what the Ph.D.,
When all departments have a place
For nincompoops like thee?

from
Each in His Season
(1993)

from Spring Suite

i.

The click
if lips slip
open, a little
ripple whispering
in your ear its warm
hints, first insinuations
till the clenched countryside
sighs and then relaxes far and wide
turning all trill, all rill and trickle
to the uttermost horizon; the winter's will
to rule, to cold control goes melting, melting,
the determined grip gone, juices rise and flow so
even the lightest breath, the faintest tempering air is
musky, all resolve dispersed, all limit liquidated in surrender.

ii.

This new growth's so faint it could be a
Will-o-the-wisp or vague idea—
First, the red sheath like a suggestion
That answers (or evades) some question;
Then, out of the black soil, green shoots
Up—as if fleeing its own roots
Or something else it must have found
Terrifying in the ground:
That generations of decay,
Corruption, death, surcharge our clay;
The hankering maggot and earthworm
We all come home to, come to term;
What cravings underlie the awesome
Thrust of seed, stem, leaf and blossom.

iii.

One warm day: the young pear tree—
a patient on a trial weekend—
ventures a stem or two, tentative
leafbuds, new color schemes; she may
forego the old restraints, that cold
solicitude of locked wards, sheets
pulled up to the chin.

A new go, all around: the meadow's
out of bankruptcy and filled with
enterprise—small field mice, moths.
Seems like we've taken on a fresh
green line of credit, vast advances
on the promise of new practices,
a sound, new management.

It's all thoroughly convincing as
a second mortgage, a second
marriage. Sap's flowing like
new currency, new lubricants.
It's plain good sense to say this
might work; history sucks; we'll
get to summer yet.

iv. A Leaf's Song

Reach; out-
stretch and over-
stress till the tuned string
sing with tension;
till the wrung taut drumhead
hum, rimshot
crack and ring;
so the guy-wired tent's skin
tense and wrack tight, distending

cable and strung tendon,
a suspension
bridge that ends
no where
but slack and empty air—
springboard, trampoline and net
to catch and bounce back
the pranking young sun
there.

vii.

Battling for the sun, young ash
and maples take up the choice
locations, shading their neighbors out.
Both crow and owl devour
each other's young, while later species
move in—swarms of convict colonists
and outcasts spread across the land.
Nestlings shrilling to be fed, the roughnecks
flourish, the smaller or more timid
are never much missed. Things
settle down; we'll be someone
respectable as the year moves on.

viii.

　　　　D'ja read me?
　　　　　　C'mere!
　　　　D'ja hear me?
　　　　　　Ya need me!

Through April's fields, small butterflies
Primp like barrettes or bright bow ties

That disappear when punk-spiked flocking
Starlings hang out, squawking, quarreling:

Don't leap for less;
            Jump my springs.
These wings, this crest
            Got everything.

In clashing yellows, oranges, greens
The land goes lewd and loud as teens
That turn up tapes, plug in this year's
Top tunes to batter at their ears:

I lose least;
Sing songs strongest.
I got lust
Lasts you longest.

Snarled in the grasses, wild strawberries
Shine bright as scabs where thick, dark hair is,
Like fireflies or the afterspark
Of roaches lit where strange cars park:

I get more faster;
            Gain most ground.
My nest's hung best.
            Don't fuck around.

In all our nubile dells and dingles
The young pulse swings, the nerve end tingles;
The same old brand new lies and jingles
Wring out the brains of Spring's worst singles:

D'ja hear me?
            C'mere!
D'ja read me?
            Ya need me!

from Summer Sequence

i.

Every young plant springing
    into heavy air,
        this flinging
one's self up, out
    from the core
        as if earth's got
too hot
    for anyone to touch
        too much;
much as the much-sung lark
    climbs higher,
        outsinging where
branches spread and flare
    like ravelled wire-
        ends or one's hair
in an electric charge might
    upstand, lift, as some
        wire prancer's parasol
might parachute and drift
    you gentle down to ground
        once more.

iii.

Up this hillside, through patches
of scrub and brush, green catches
on as fire or virus spreads
through unsuspecting heads —
a new belief, the fashion
and excuse for passion.

These towering beeches crowd
on foliage like a proud
ship's canvas that must fear,
still envious, still near,
those vessels it's outrun
for its place in the sun.

Our orchard, woods and meadow
now breathe out the credo
and pieties of growth;
those who've survived seem loath
to find luxuriance less
than fit reward and progress.

Even the ongoing brook
can't spare nerve now to look
back at what's been drowned,
what's gaining on it, bound
to jail it up at last —
the dry bones of its past.

iv.

As cock orioles lock
        beaks and, orange
                slash-and-dart wings
battering, flail the sky;
        as flyweight fighter-
                pilot, laser-
throated humming-
        birds climb each
                above each other
then dive down, drive
        each other off; fierce,
                piercing as the arc
of an acetylene torch,
        or the hand-struck
                spark that might

ignite and scorch the eye,
      here the buck bunting,
           indigo, his million
prisms scattering
      shattered white light
           blue, blue, blue
homes in through
      the startled air,
           a tracer or some
riled-up, forge-
      bright rivet
           to its mark.

viii. Cabbage Butterflies

Paired like square vanes
      spinning in some sun-
           spun, glass-globed top,
they orbit their closed
      system, lifting off
           the meadow grasses
high and higher and
      then flutter down
           apart, yet rejoined,
climb twirling like
      a bolo's ends, as twin
           stars or ice skaters
csardas, caught in
      one another's gravity
           till all earth's
greater weight winds
      every urge and engine
           down. Why don't
      we go
upstairs?

ix.

Deregulated summer rolls on:
Our meadow's making hay as if
    the national gross product must be
grass; the duty of all flesh: get high
    as your eye by the Fourth of July.

Fledged, open-eyed, the rough young
bluejays squall like soccer fans
    crammed in their twiggy stadium—loud
disciples of some rock star, cure-all
    politics or new saviour: greed.

Nothing will come of nothing; things
lead to things: the ad campaign's still
    on though the summer's till brims over.
Sunflowers smile down like visitors
    to Plato's Cave or brazen bank examiners,

where shameless, coarse young leaves spread
open to the sun. Through ditch and hedgerow
    kudzu carries out its hostile
takeover; the greenback reigns. Our
    scriptures: lovecharts, popcharts and the Dow.

x.

The loitering red-tail screeches,
    Redoubled in the pond,
Then tools off down the valley and
    Beyond, beyond, beyond . . .

Locust and katydid grind on
    Like the whirr where distant foundries
Work all three shifts. Thick brambles spread
    Over all known boundaries.

Fireflies, rising in the fields, blip
    The darkening screen to chart
Another ring laid on the trees,
    More fat around the heart.

from Autumn Variations

i.

The evening grosbeak on the lawn
Will turn his back on us, move on
With his wide family and those friends
We thought were ours. That's how it ends.
If it's been good, be glad it's been;
It won't be. The cold shoulder's in.
We must make do, once summer's done,
With our fair weather friends or none.

ii.

The garden's garter snake,
the warty toad in our garage
don't get around these days.
Woodchuck and rabbit sink
into themselves; if they
have some idea, who's to say?
The few birds left accept
the mob opinions
and the fashions: a dull
Stalinist grey that will
offend no one. The turtles
turntail on the pond, withdraw
to meditate, regroup or,
joining what's too big to beat,
dig down in the numb
security of clay, one
with their fate.

iii.

In spray-paint, psychedelic, gaudy,
Fall scrawls its name—a blunt and bawdy
Challenge to the complacent wood.
We say: there goes the neighborhood;
It is not and it cannot come to good.
Soon, flustered leaves will sag like torn
Wallpaper; solid dark walls, worn
Through here and there, expose a bitter
Sky while, on the bare ground, litter
And stub ends pile up everywhere.
Not even one green plant would dare
Poke its nose out in that crude air
Of catch-as-catch-can thievery, lust,
Cut-throat protection and sick trust.
Where year by year we walked together
Determined paths, a wilder atmosphere
Wheels in, flaunting its chains, blades and black leather.

iv.

Imperial greenery withdraws,
flamboyant and corrupt; the leaf's
far government's lost
faith in its mission, that certainty
to be despotic and
victorious. Now failure's
certain, a certain
mercy enters in; such as
it is, the sun
gets spread around, the magnanimity
of the poor. Only some pines,
hard-needled loyalists, cling
to their colors and won't change. Dark,
under those implacable branches,
nothing grows.

vi.

Sharp, black crickets
have got the house
surrounded; miners and sappers
gnaw our siding;
buckwheat flies, wasps
and spiders—spies—
thread the cellar and the walls.
And these are the deserters
who've lost the front
outside. Put on fat;
put on fur; the windows
rattle. The only news
says we'll know soon
what sort of man you are.

viii.

Bare bones! Bare bones!
is the wind's suggestion
and, one by one, leaves
like bright embroidery
rinsed in bleach or like
words in the brain's skein,
the tree of memory,
are gone. All sweet details
pass on in "the abstraction
of old age": skeletal
trunk and branchings, lacy
tracework of each leaf,
medulla and the neural reach
of those ways we once knew
things we forget
under the soft, featureless
democracy of snow.

from Snow Songs

i.

one. now another. one
more. some again; then done.
though others run
down your windshield when
up ahead a sudden
swirl and squall comes on
like moths, mayflies in a swarm
against your lights, a storm
of small fry, seeds, unknown
species, populations. every one
particular and special; each one
melting, breaking, hurling on
into the blank black. soon
never to be seen again.
most never seen.
all, gone.

ii.

First, the exhausted brown
leaves, then the snow comes down
the way a year's change shakes
hairs loose or those dull flakes
littering your shoulder.
Soon, windier and colder
gusts—as confetti falls
on our sunstruck festivals,
then, flurrying wilder, thicker,
scatters like heavy ticker-

tape over the parade
route and the motorcade
of some departing hero.
Now, into a near-zero
visibility
where nothing can be
known sure of events,
what with the pervasive, dense
smother of shredded documents.

iii.

White out; white out; so
    that the landscape's ledger
        balances again.
On the hill, the white-tailed deer's
    remains are spirited
        away like laundered funds:
flesh, pelt and all
    the inner workings nibbled
        down, salted away inside
the general, unmentionable,
    unseen economy of the woods.
        Bones, like the broken branches,
soften, sink back down
    in ground that sent them
        out to reconnoiter.
Soon this whole, broad
    Stalingrad will be no more
        than scattered fading photographs,
just some aging soldiers'
    recollections till at last
        all thought dies down to the
perfection of the blank page
    and the lighted
        screen that will flick off.

vi.

Now snow lies level
    with the windowsills. Along
the thruway, traffic
    like fresh water flows
between banks ten feet
    above our heads. Still
it sifts down slow
    as infinite, small
skeletons of diatoms drift,
    settling through the salt seas,
falling only inches year
    by year, some 20,000 species,
geometric, crystalline, no
    two shells alike, covering
the sea's floor hundreds
    of feet deep. Now turn
the radio up louder; try to
    catch the local dialect.

viii.

Leaving the snow
    bank, your boot leaves
        a fossil print—an
emptiness remains. Just so,
    across the field you've made
        a trail of vacancies.
    Still the snow
falls—as a clean sheet smooths
    your shape out of the bed
    you don't go back to.
        You are the missing
    tooth, the one place
at the table, lost

wax from the casting—though,
while they last,
these chicken scratchings hold
the voice unspoken on
the finished page as under
plaster hardening,
a fading face.

Birds Caught, Birds Flying

I handed you, for you to hold—
as a surgeon some live tissue—
the chickadee that had slipped through
our open window, then went
fluttering, blundering around
our walls. While we processioned
room to room with it, you felt
it pulsing, shivering against
that tender cage of fingers. Outside,
you stroked its back once, took
your hand away; upraised there
on the altar of your palm, it sat
still, blinking, till it knew it
had survived, and flew away.

Two years after you left, I came
back to this locked house; starlings
had been down the chimney. They must
have circuited—dark ghosts—the cold
abandoned rooms, dodged among
our furnishings, gone battering
against the lightning flash of panes
as a neurotic goes on battering
at habits he can't break.
Then died down. I found
one drowned in the toilet, one
behind the bed—mere white bones
in a wreath by their own feathers.
Mice or maggots took all else.

In the marketplace at San Miguel
once, I bought a sparrow hawk
that fainted at my touch. Kept
only overnight, those bright wings

flashed toward the morning's jacarandas.
Now, hummingbirds that snare themselves
high in our garage's dormer,
chickadees that knock themselves
against our windows—they peer
out through our arched fingers like
a transplant between ribs.
We stroke them, once, to life again,
and watch them go on, on their way
again then, when they must be gone.

Elena Ceauçescu's Bed

Making ourselves at home in that broad bed
    Elena left, we slept snug as the mouse
That, burrowing in guest room blankets, fed
    Her brood last winter in our summer house.

What bed, through all our lives long, had we known
    If not the tyrant's? How many had been driven
Homeless and hungering while I had my own
    Bed, my own room? How many have been given

Lives at hard labor while our markets rose
    And we had all we asked for in the lands
Of milk and honey? Where could you find those
    Who hunted, once, that hill where my house stands?

There'll be just one bed, too soon, for us all.
    What empire's hacked out by the meek, the kind?
The lioness kills; the lion feasts; the small
    Bury their noses in what's left behind.

In Memory of Lost Brain Cells

—on receiving an honorary doctorate from Allegheny College, 5/19/91.

Here, at our Academic Festival,
It's right that we survivors should recall

Those lost from our ranks: bold, selfless neurons
Questioned and persecuted past endurance;

Our agents, gatherers of intelligence
Whose networks through benighted continents

Flashed out curt messages of wit and brilliance
Till marked, seized, whisked away, wiped out by millions,

Never to be replaced. Still, those connections
They formed live on in spite of past defections,

In spite of new betrayals, quislings, quitters.
Others fill in, take up where old transmitters

Shut down. Daily we see more territory
Fall prey to new world orders, to *a priori*

Systems or pressure groupies, find more knowledge
Banned by the thought police, see one more college

Sold out to fixed theories, one more liar
Voted to high office, one more supplier

Of comfy truths belaurelled; each night some drunken
Purge wipes out our cells, leaves us with shrunken

Heads, brains laundered, safe but uninstructed,
One more priceless faculty deconstructed.

Still, who would live in any times but these?
These are the days that try men's synapses,

Nights when we learn what axons and dendrites
Through our dark hemispheres switch on the lights.

We veterans of the brain's unCivil War—
I pray thee ask not one man, one cell more—

We few, we happy few must bless our lot.
What difference if our old professors thought

To grant our doctorate "wouldn't be prudent,"
We can still hope to snag one through a student.

You supersnoops and spies, that CIA
Whose postings keep us live and human, stay

True to your codes of cortical responses,
Facts all men need though none believes he wants us.

Though names, dates, facts fall from our memory,
Stand fast: we shall live through this third degree.

Not all nerves fail; hold your cerebral mission;
This happy day shall doctor our condition.

An Envoi, Post-TURP

(After Trans-Urethral Resectioning of the Prostate, men experience retrograde ejaculation, the semen being passed later during urination.)

Farewell, children of my right hand and bliss.
You'll come no more but in bright streams of piss,
Never more turn my bedroom towels stiff,
Whitewash the walls or glisten on the quiff;
Never more swim like salmon or rough Norse
Invaders swarming upstream to the source.
Once, ovaries were ovaries; sperms, sperms.
In nine short months you brought us all to terms
When captive loins were sentenced by your court
To long years, lawyers' fees and child support.
You cared for just one thing—aye, that's the rub:
Each of you, at your Health and Country Club
Timed training laps, did pushups by the pool
Shunning each voice that cried, "Back, back you fools,
We'll all be killed—it's a blow job!" You hurled
Yourselves, bluff hardy semen, on the world
Like Noah's load that crested with the Flood
To populate the land and stand at stud.
Ink of my pen, you words spent ἐν ἀρχῇ,
This writer, knowing all he's cast away,
Knowing your creamy genes and DNA
Encodes our texts, pirates and then reprints us, says,
"Good night, bad cess to you, sweet prince and princesses."

A Curse

— *against A. H., who does not make instruments.*

You drove off with the applewood
From that great, bounteous tree that stood
Lightning-battered and storm-tortured
Half a century in our orchard
And whose trunk, 20 feet tall, grew
Hard, dark-toned and 2 feet through
Then, seasoning for 10 years, had lain
Waiting a purpose worth its grain;
You took, besides, our walnut, spruce
And cherry boards for your own use
And warm ivory we'd soaked loose
From piano keys. Grave as a goose,
You gave your promise to produce
An instrument, made an excuse
Instead, then sure as self-abuse,
One more excuse, one more, one yet
Till we both knew that's all we'd get.

Now, if you sell that harpsichord
May the straightgrained spruce of its soundboard,
Warping and twisting, wrench apart
So irritable buzzings start
To breed inside that lengthening crack
And pins slip—not enough to slack
Strings though the true pitch won't quite hold.
There, where you signed your name in gold
May random checking split and etch it
Straight through the words, *A. H. Me Fecit.*

Or if you keep it as your own,
May it ring with a strong, clean tone
At times. But when in public may

Jacks swell and jam so that you play
Garbles of chord and melodies
Gapped like decaying teeth or cheese.
May felts fail so each error lingers
Long in the ear and may your fingers
Slip off the ivory, slick as wax,
So you play always in the cracks
Between keys that go limp or stick,
Tearing your nail down to the quick.

May all you set your hand to, buckle,
Breaking your finger at the knuckle
Which, aging, aching, goes rheumatic,
Turns your recorder holes asthmatic,
Your fiddle feeble and your squeeze
Box troubled by a sleazy wheeze.
May your drum rhythms stumble and alter
So that the dancers halt, start, falter,
And when you lift your voice, may it wobble
As if you'd told things not quite probable.

May far-flung audiences recognize
Just what you are. And may the wise
Try your virginals, guess at their price,
Look long but think best not to ask it,
Seeing its form's so like a casket
He could go to the boneyard in it
Before you finished him his spinet.

Still, may no formal punishment
Ease your guilt; may each day be spent
Evading lawyers' calls or tax
Inspectors. Falling shy on facts,
On good faith or harmonic rules,
Be fearless around power tools.
Should you pick up some stranger's kit
Or fine wood, switch on your drill bit;
If you should skirt around a law,

Look up once from your band saw;
If you should ever break your faith
May loose hairs tangle in your lathe.

Lastly, may those you trust in break
Their word and for their own sweet sake
Waste your gifts on things to make
Them comfy till the day you die.
Every midnight may you lie
Awake with one who'll scorn and rule
You for a coward and a fool.
That is, I hope you spend your life
Alone—or better, with your wife.

from In Flower

i. Snow Drops

Spring's first whispers
Though in winter's tongue:
Frosty globes hung above green
Leaves and thawed ground like
Lamps left on all day
To tell us dark and cold
Are never far
And neither green nor gold
Nor icy white can stay
Here long. Or stay away.

iv. Dandelions

Some Viking's blond shock;
　　　　one sun-flare of a whetted edge
across our suburban's clipped lawn;
　　　　one settler, two, and then
the grey-haired, smoke-soft afterburst
　　　　remains: a spook transmitter
disperses intermittent sniping
　　　　till the whole broad yard erupts
in small arms fire, the firing
　　　　off of neurons through the brain's
dark networks, and the field
　　　　is taken.

v. Bearded Iris

All labial folds and ripples
    like the wavy edge of some
        Victorian candy dish,
the ridges of brain coral or
    flamenco dancer's hemline
        flared out, arching overhead,
the lapping shawl and mantle
    of a manta ray, these petals,
bearded, curling as a wet,
        warm tongue spreads smoothing,
    soothing all refusal
down.

vi. Touch-Me-NOT

Jewelweed, gem-set
or enamelled basket
earrings, light wired,
dazzling at some dancer's
cheek and soft throat,
inviting, offering
NOTHING
to the hand;
still tossing in the
warmed breeze beckoning to
Stand Back
Close!

xi. Daylilies

First, like a kid who understands
or sure thinks sure he knows the answers,
one shoots up a swaggering hand

demanding the teacher's eye
then another and another try
for places in the sun, give high-
fives and get mobbed in triumph by
the team, gang, clan, the green nation
all elation, jubilation, celebration,
parading colors, slogans, gas balloons
as light as empty speech clouds in cartoons
or more like surrendering platoons
that (Hands Up!), frightened,
fall back to the dirt, the night.

xii. Black Columbine

Green sprouts outbursting every
which way, begonias and pansies
flaunting reds and purples—the garden's
gang flags. And at the center,
one black columbine, not quite
like Morgenstern's dark star (the infamous
daynightlamp which, one switch being flicked,
transfigured any day, however
bright, to perfect night)—more like
a cockeyed hatstand hung with
witches' caps or old-time widows' bonnets
in memory of everything that's going
or else gone. Above all, like
some sort of antimatter or a negative
of what might be developed, then fixed here,
and then live a little.

New Poems

The Discreet Advantages of a Reichstag Fire

Those who do not learn history are doomed to repeat it.
—Santayana

No accident, no natural catastrophe
Can advance your mission. Storms, earthquakes
Or flash floods can stir up short-term sympathies, making
Mere neighbors believe they could be friends. Obviously,
Casualties of those disasters will crave no retaliation
For what some god's determined or an impartial
Nature. Nothing but willed injuries can secure us all
In rancor dead-set against an alien folk or nation

As yet unspecified—one blessed, though, by resources
You aspire to, or bases situated for attacking
Those who have. One reassuring factor is any lack
Of the latest minute's weaponry or well-trained forces.
Make much, though, of some obscure menacings: forbidden
Stores of nerve gas, plans drawn up for chemical or germ
Assault. Herr Goering said, "Red sympathizers—we have firm
Proof—keep high explosives stockpiled and well hidden."

Your first stroke is to require from your Reichstag a Decree
For the Protection of the People and the State;
Once that's locked in, a second Law that Alleviates
The Misery of the People, though termed officially
The Enabling Act—mitigating thus the suspension
Of free speech, press and assembly, while condoning
Search, seizure, opened mail, tapped wires and phones
Or wounds acquired in limit-free "protective detention."

The Reichstag silenced, look down with a calm contempt
On schemes subjecting your designs to higher orders
Or outworn treaties. No land on this earth has a border

Or air space sealed against your clear right to preempt
And rectify. You may be forced to jail or execute
Some you've conquered but who still thwart your commands;
There's one triumph can console you: in your homeland
Your whim is law and your least wish absolute.

Talking Heads

TV's hand puppets don't ooze out one word
These days about Iraq's oil. That can be taken
For granted. Anyone tuned-in will have heard
Strong-arm democracy brings home the bacon.
Once we've inflicted freedom and secured
Men's good will, we'll sleep sound, dream right, then wake

To heaped-up platters. Nobody's been forbidden
To mention things that nobody dares think—
That's honor among thieves. Loot, once hidden,
Can still be leached off quicker than a wink.
Where's your cut of the stash gone? Check your eyelids:
Sly thieves and robber barons never blink.

Slick puppet masters have to keep count who's
Made a killing and who's been double-crossed
To bury that on the dark side of the news,
The brain's recycle bin. True recall might cost
Friends, income, or a life too good to lose.
Analysts sometimes ask how decent Germans,
Facing a sudden scarcity of Jews,
Maintained their ignorance of the Holocaust:
None mentions just how many we let squirm
And twist at rope's end for their predetermined,
Preemptive wars. But then, of course, they lost.

Gringolandia

It's what Hungary was for the Viennese
or Romania for old Romans; those who
were once filthy rich can still afford
to be dissatisfied and surly; the retired
or failed can get creative with their past
and resurrect as actors, painters, poets
—like Socrates or CEOs in prison;
those who've never in their lives been
hungry can advocate fantastic diets
or lecture on The Hungers of Our Times.

We are all born-agains through the wonders
of conversion, perjury or cosmetic surgery.
One ingénue may have had three face lifts,
each one following a will or a new alimony.
The play's director, (also head of the
town's Odd Fellows) cancelled the opening,
flying to Hong Kong for a shipment of cocaine.
Our friendly neighborhood murderer is giving
up his weekly column, "Jailhouse Cooking,"
to open an antique shop with his mother.

The rich come for two weeks every year
at least, visiting trophy mansions, their own
museums to a life someone almost like them
must have lived. As for living,
the servants do that for them. Housemaids
wash and hand-iron the unsullied bedsheets,
or on vast, bare tables arrange the cut flowers
that the gardener's just gardened. Upstairs,
bedlights and radios flick themselves off or on
in warning: somebody could be home.

The natives prove useful: giving us occasions
for good works and those inspiring causes
that fill up long, do-nothing days. Although
we do scold any neighbor who overpays them,
there is something we must still admire
in how we forgive them for inbred dishonesties,
(*"Why call the police?*—they *of all people know!"*)
Let us invite the best few to parties, expound
indigenous mythologies to them and commend
strong home lives as the alternative to migration.

On the Streets

i.

> Scary,
either one of them alone. But
together on that run-down corner:
the young black, thick-set, the older white,
shock-headed, crookbacked, shaking
his cane at some car passing.
I crossed the street. Then, though—
was it a windbreak?—thick cardboard,
carpeting on the sidewalk, where someone
must have spent the night—
I turned back with my loose change.
"Oh, no sir. Don't
need one thing. I got disability—
get 1500 dollars every month."

ii.

Crouched down to the buckled concrete
she'd swept first with brown paper,
then buffed with her fist,
she folds a yellow cotton blouse,
left sleeve over, right sleeve next,
hem end folded up, neck end down;
then lays it out
> as if in a showcase.
Tugs up out of her shoulder bag
a long skirt, flowery, shakes it,
holds it to her waist, refolds it;
one belt, one T-shirt, odd ends of cloth
sorted, counted, smoothed, and then
restored to their right place.

All's well; substantial.
                    Will not accept
the orange you're holding out to her.
Go closer and she'll sheer off,
trusting her bare feet to see her safe
across the cobblestones, glass
shatters, dog shit, bent beer cans,
still cradling to her chest one
gilded, high-heeled party sandal.

Sleeps, nights, in a neighbor's
yard nearby, some distance
from her family's. Speaks to
no one
          who'd known her then.

iii.

Proud
          of the meager Spanish
I could manage, I offered,
"No tengo cambio"
                    in excuse.
Peering up through lenses
thick as signal lanterns
frosted, long sunk underseas,
she shot out one claw,
snapping,
          "Go to the bank, then,"
in good English.
                    Which I did.

Lady!—

in lane, out, veering
past eighteen-wheelers eighty-
five or ninety, reading
that true romance or new
true gospel propped right-angled
on you steering wheel along
this 8-lane turnpike to
some crucial contract meeting,
some catechism class, your grown
kid's high school graduation
or some far-off impatient
lover—don't go fumbling
after maps or for your cell phone
for directions; such destinations
recede from you or crumble;
don't wave your free hand to
dry your nails or pull askew
the rearview mirror to repair
your lipstick, eye paint, hairdo—
and even if your goal stands firm,
it isn't likely you'll arrive
at that Good Book's good juicy parts
in which he gets her and kind hearts
lap up virtue's wages;
nonetheless, those fixed pages
wait for you, unfaltering,
mandatory, unaltered
as carved stone slabs, and just so
we do our housework, homework,
to the tunes and credos of
Soap-Oprahland, make love,
make money or make war
to the half-forgotten morals from

film scripts whose musics hum
in our numbed skulls forevermore
and, while we're human, don't do
just what we do; this world's not what
this world's cracked up to be or what
we're cranked up and then cracked up for.

At the Villa

Sun-glazed waters, calm ahead. Our boat's wake
Spreading behind us like a rumor, shudders
the stateliest mansions mirrored on the lake.
     Water polluted: Swim at your own risk.

When we take drinks out on the terraced lawn
Under the azalea hedges, dragonflies
Hover like alien choppers, then seem gone.
     Did a door just slam, back there in the house?

Along the paths and walkways, between bricks
And faults in rock walls, small lizards dash,
Dark zigzags, little black lightning streaks.
     The weather persists—relentlessly sublime.

The peacock feathers scattered by some beast
Near the front gate, the lion's crushed stone nose,
Stumps gapping the lines of staunch old chestnut trees . . .
     In our hard times, we've said, "I don't deserve this!"

And then righteously pronounced our curses
On the rich and privileged. Wouldn't we deserve
Those same curses, if our fates had been reversed?
     Don't bad things happen to *unlucky* people, too?

Farm Kids

Our neighbor's slim rag doll of a daughter (not,
we're told, of his own getting) breathed out: "You've got
so many cookbooks!"—each eye a startled O
as it skimmed our kitchen shelves—"And so
much food!" Later, straight-faced, she said her mother
lives now with her new boyfriend in another
county. Hard up for farm jobs, her "Dad" has to drive
60 miles to the factory, getting up at 5
AM to leave them where his folks watch after them
until he gets back home—sometimes 5 PM.

We go for long walks every evening. If we pass
their trailer, they all tumble out shouting, "Snodgrass!
Snodgrass!" The slim, straight-faced one is thought slow
by her teachers. There's much she'd do well not to know.
The cool offspring of our city friends are driven
to special schools, sports dates, parties, given
phones, computers, cars, the insatiate stuff
that will guarantee they can't ever get enough.
Our neighbors' less keen hungers and kinder drives
make sure they'll make nothing of their lives but lives.

Leavings

Foolish, frugal Mrs. Mousie, why
would you accept our generous offer, why
trust our least word ever, why
take these green crumbs from our bait trays,
bit by bit, bite by bite, for safe deposit
in this Romanian black clay vase
of things already too good to be true?

How long were you abuilding, how
long since, this unnumbered Swiss account,
your private smack stash, closed portfolio
of Security and Nourishment,
Sound Ideas for an Easy Mind?
Poor pirate, without chart or map's X
we've turned up your best treasure.

No trace of you, though, or your pink
nurslings. Our fierce thirsts drove you
back out to the fields whose hungers
you'd once fled, where if you became
some fox's protein or coyote's bit,
you can pass on this Pharaoh's curse—
our taint still seeping through the territory.

On High

As the day-laborers in our loft pried loose
the slivery, hand-split lath and gray,
unpainted plaster, it all came showering down
on their bent heads like Jahveh's judgments
or Zeus's gold streams on the naked Danaë:
dead flies, snakeskins, bat shit, a boy's clodhopper,
The *Christian Messenger* for 1902,
sex magazines, a gnarled cane, then a cat's
carcass—a tattered fur sack
flapped around the bones and fanged skull, all
fat and tissues gone. Heavy, heavy
what hung over, long years, like an angel's perch
or sniper blind, bare inches from our heads!
Say, a tramp cat crept in out of whetted winds,
snarled in some dark cranny, the dead flesh
nibbled off by its past prey, mice. Or battered
by some farm child, revenge on his rough parents,
then buried where no one could see. The workmen,
smirking, must have wedged it back in overhead,
their detector watchcat against cold forces, the dread
that goes with us, *Take the key and lock her up,
My fair Lady*, unsuspecting converts adhering
to the ancient sacrifice: "Thou cast-off cat of
catastrophes, calvaries, scapecat, lar and caretaker
spokescat, O be kind!" in our new ceiling's
2x4s and plywood to which we do not lift our eyes.

Song Slam

What heavenly chorister, what angel voice
hails me, hushed, into my living room?
                    A birdie with a yellow bill
        a lemon yellow back as well, black cap,
                white and black wingflaps,
    a goldfinch, uncaged
Sprach zu mir ein lust'ge Fink
            bel canto soloist of our seed feeder
                    sings for his supper
    or—now hear this!—for his retort
to our boombox's Bach Cantata,
            "Singet den Herr'n ein Neues Lied,"
    answering each soprano phrase
                    pos d'auzel chanton lor for
with improvised cadenzas
            Non es meravelha s'eu chan
            melh de nulh autre chantador
    in cantabile obligato backchat,
                    zidiwick, zificigo, zificigo, zificigo,
            wild canary shrill, contrary scat-chant
    Anything you can sing
        I can sing better
                until some sudden start has
        sent him back off on his own and sent me
            Der Vogelfaenger bin ich ja
                back to my own perch to write.

Ruffed Grouse

Just three weeks ago our Trade Towers crashed;
now you, a full-grown, ruffed male grouse—
shy, undercover drummer from our woods—
rammed headlong into our picture window, lay
throbbing in the sideyard grass, then died.
Poor numbskull kamikaze, intent on no crusade
more splendid than the capture of a drowsy
housefly or some dowdy mate! No glory-
granting Grousegod, no Virgin's dive-bomb dove
made you an offer too good to be true, proposed
some higher aim, some heaven's henfold plumped by houris,
some new field theory cornering the meadow's market.
No airy self-reflection—Jahveh, Allah, Jesus, Baal—
rose up in our overbloating glass gladhanding you;
only these earthbound, bunco-brained high-fliers,
raptors stooping to pluck out your fanned tailfeathers
then traipse back about our own affairs.

Who Steals My Good Name

*—for that person who obtained my debit card number and
spent $11,000 in five days*

My pale stepdaughter, just off the schoolbus,
Scowled, "Well, that's the last time I say my name's
Snodgrass!" Just so, may that anonymous
Mexican male who prodigally claims

My clan lines, identity and the sixteen
Digits that unlock my bank account
Think twice. This less than proper name's been
Taken by three ex-wives, each for an amount

Past all you've squandered, each more than pleased
To change it back. That surname you affect
May have more consequences than getting teased
By dumb kids or tracked down by bank detectives.

Don't underrate its history: one of ours played
Piano on his prison's weekly broadcast;
One got rich on a scammed quiz show; one made
A bungle costing the World Series. My own past

Could subject you to guilt by association:
Should you write anything beyond false checks,
Abandon all hope of large press publication
Or prizes—critics shun that name like sex

Without a condom. Whoever steals my purse
Helps chain me to my writing desk again
For fun and profit. Take thanks, then, with my curse:
May your pen name help send you to *your* pen.

Nocturnes

---

i.

Leave your glasses there where you lost them,
    Now a wider blindness spreads;
Turn out hearing aids, all tapes, all radios;
    Sow silence with its kinder song.

Let the oak and maple trees make up
    Their differences, hedgerow and meadow
Spill over, absorbed in one another.
    While full dark washes in, sanding
Down the land's cursed edges, washing over
    Clouded glass, the cracked shell, washing out
All borders and particulars, leave
    A world for lacewings and the luna moth.

Now let the mole, the vole and the fieldmouse
    Pause, vagrant in the unmown hay;
Let the dim path, that we took so long
    To wear away, recover in the deepening grass.

ii.

Seen from higher up, it makes its first move
in the low creekbed, the marshlands
down the valley, spreading across the open
hayfields, the hedgerows with their tops
still lit, laps the roadbed, flows over
lawns and gardens, past the house and up
the wooded hillside back behind us
till only some few rays still scythe
between the treetrunks from the far horizon
and are gone.

Down close, it seeps up
from the grass's roots, oozes
out from under flat stones and weedstalks,
then climbs the crevassed ash and oak bark
to the leaves that all day soaked in sun
till flash and highlights dim like whitecaps
clasped, becalmed in night.

Here, darkness never falls;
we raise our own.

iii.

From the blocked-up chimney's side
they slip out, bursting into dingy air

**his open black face forming
his grin again**

from the unpainted, nailed-down shutters,
from soffits, the roof's cornicepiece

*her flurried skirtpleats
twirling, flared out*

crisscross, and skittering helter-
skelter through the tree's limbs,

**his legs churning, reversing,
slicing through the broken field**

they sideslip, flutter and glide
tip, dip, and then dive down,

*white, the slipstrap clung
to her young, flushed shoulder*

recovering, maneuvering
over fresh-cut meadow grasses

**or coiled in the huge tuba walked
side by side to school with me**

then up to the garage's dormer, back
to the dark loft, the black attic

*whom I would never once
dare kiss or touch*

to fold up wings, to fold away
their dead selves for another night.

iv. Night Voices

Clear out here
you don't hear screams, shots, chants
of mobs raging, ambulances
or fire sirens;
maybe some rabbit a fox caught,
some young bird squirming in a cat's
jaws or the clenched claws
of an owl. Otherwise,
the outstretched countryside lies
still. Until
here in my bedroom's wall-
absorbing darkness, one small
cheep insists that sleep
is inappropriate for anyone
whose lifelong insomnia will be done
too soon—
my discarded wristwatches' thin
alarms whose instructions have been
lost, while unexhausted
batteries, lurking where they're buried

in my drawer of outworn underwear,
      survive to drive
them wide awake again
like closed networks in the brain:
      these memories
of some that you once loved who'd never care
to hear from you, of questions you'd scarce dare
      hear, of what fear
underlay those days you used all wrong
or didn't use. Just how long
      can shrieks growing so weak
still carry on? We'll learn, no doubt,
which of us can longest last this out.

v.

at hearing's far edge,
      cricket
lonely, from the dark hedgerow
      or horizon, to our closet's
      mate or to fate's callback
      CRACK IT

down the valley's marshlands:
      creak,
the whirring of spring peepers;
      tiny millworks—the shrill
night heron's shriek or bullfrog's
      CROAK

against the blind trees' screen
      blink
      inconstant constellations;
fireflies fix on their own kind's
      winking high signs, then go
      BLANK

vi. At Home, Lost

Awake, opening your eyes, you can see
nothing.
           Nothing.
                    On your feet, you start
toward the bathroom and bang into a blank wall.
Turning, you skin your ankle on a chest.
As if someone in the night had turned your bed around
or transposed the furniture and hallways. Reaching
for the light switch you fumble at the inside of a closet.
You've become the blind mime or some fly
between the screen and windowglass.

> *"For every hundred prisoners leave*
> *one eye and let them walk home."*

On hands and knees, touching your bed's end,
crawl back in and start over.
                      Maybe Earth's
magnetic North or moral imperatives are shifting. Maybe
you ought to do this every other night
by way of practicing.

vii.

Square by square, bright windows,
Flick on in all the towns—lit
Picture frames but vacant. Here,
Down sun-forsaken streets, his effigies
Hang, sacred, celebrant on every lamppost.

In the far heights, ten million splinters
Recollect the shivered dome of the day.

Then dawn seeps through. Grackles, black
Anthracite blasted from the pit, break
Loose and scatter over glowing lawns,
Fresh orchards, garden beds. Their wings,
Gang flags, will be rallying here soon.

Nightwatchman's Song

—*after Heinrich I. F. Biber*

i.

What's unseen may not exist—
Or so those secret powers insist
   That prowl past nightfall,
Enabled by the brain's blacklist
   To fester out of sight.

So we streak from bad to worse
Through an expanding universe
   And see no evil.
On my rounds like a night nurse
   Or sentry on *qui vive*,

I make, through murkier hours, my way
Where the sun patrolled all day
   Toward stone-blind midnight
To poke this flickering flashlamp's ray
   At what's hushed up and hidden.

Lacking all leave or protocol,
Things, one by one, hear my footfall,
   Blank out their faces,
Dodge between trees, find cracks in walls
   Or lock down offices.

Still, though scuttling forces flee
Just as far stars recede from me
   To outmost boundaries,
I stalk through ruins and debris,
   Graveyard and underground.

Led by their helmetlantern's light,
Miners inch through anthracite;
    I'm the unblinking mole
That sniffs out what gets lost or might
    Slip down the world's black hole.

ii.

(tipsy, the watchman returns, ending his rounds)

What's obscene?—just our obsessed,
Incessant itch and interest
    In things found frightful:
In bestial tortures, rape, incest;
    In ripe forbidden fruit

Dangling, lush, just out of reach;
Dim cellars nailed up under each
    Towering success,
The loser's envy that must teach
    A fierce vindictiveness,

The victor's high court that insures
Pardon for winners and procures
    Little that's needed
But all we lust for. What endures?—
    Exponential greed

And trash containers overflowing
With shredded memos, records showing
    What, who, when, why
'til there's no sure way of knowing
    What's clear to every eye:

The heart's delight in hatred, runny
As the gold drip from combs of honey;
   The rectal intercourse
Of power politics and money
   That slimes both goal and source.

What's obscured?—what's abscessed.
After inspection, I'd suggest
   It's time we got our head
Rewired. I plan to just get pissed,
   Shitfaced and brain-dead.

Chasing Fireflies

—for McGraw and Marvell

You live bits of the first Big Bang
Burning to turn each other on
As Yin winks to rekindle Yang,
Or ships blink Morse glinting the murk,
Let crusted contact points be drawn
To contact points, then close the circuit.

Gilt specks in my prospector's pan,
Flecks in Night's lapis lazuli,
Midsummer's flickering Xmas strings
Whose random constellations can
Alter our sky-signs' augury,
Linking up dots to outline Things,

I am the mower, Snodgrass, known
Through fields and meadows run to seed,
Undertended and overgrown
With ragweed, sneezewort and neglect,
Where moths lay eggs and fireflies breed—
You are the harvest I collect.

Forgive the finger rings we children
Forged from your torsos' fading brilliance;
Join in my Mason jar, this glass
That lucidates dark worlds when filled
With your good kith and kin whose millions
Might excite, once, critical mass.

I've loafed all summer at my lawn
Chirping songs bawdy and improper;
Now that my chords are halfway gone,

Leaving me like some dumb grasshopper
Whose half-cracked brain may never mend,
Let axon still ping out to dendrite.

Enter my net and neural network,
You sparks that arc old synapses;
Though I've grown stiff and gray and can't learn
New songs or finger the same fretwork,
You wouldn't leave Diogenes'
Ghost out here looking for his lantern?

Fast Foods: A Rap Rondeau

With fast foods you've got to feast since you can't fast—
    In next to no time you feel famished, though
You're looking fat-haunched, paunchy and flab-assed
And by now, the force-fed figure you've amassed
    Hamstrings your frame. Getting enough comes slow
      With fast foods.

    Like fast fucking. Simone Weil warned: we know
Appetites from addictions by an acrid contrast
In their satisfactions: that is, by how long they last.
    You *can* get too much bread; there is no
Such thing as enough cocaine. Hungers turn vast
As lunar landscapes where you range, aghast
    At your own emptiness. With time, those faux
Fixes that should fill lust's vacuums cast
    -rate you: both flesh and flesh's cravings grow
      With fast foods.

Lasting

"Fish oils," my doctor snorted, "and oily fish
are actually good for you. What's actually wrong
for anyone your age are all those dishes
with thick sauce that we all pined for so long
as we were young and poor. Now we can afford
to order such things, just not to digest them;
we find what bills we've run up in the stored
plaque and fat cells of our next stress test."

My own last test scored in the top 10 percent
of males in my age bracket. Which defies
all consequence or justice—I've spent
years shackled to my desk, saved from all exercise.
My dentist, next: "Your teeth seem quite good
for someone your age, better than we'd expect
with so few checkups or cleanings. Teeth should
repay you with more grief for such neglect"—

echoing how my mother always nagged,
"Brush a full 100 strokes," and would jam
cod liver oil down our throats till we'd go gagging
off to flu-filled classrooms, crammed
with vegetables and vitamins. By now,
I've outlasted both parents whose plain food
and firm ordinance must have endowed
this heart's tough muscle—weak still in gratitude.

Parents

In their cramped but mist-bright bathroom,
Tucked in white, fresh Sunday towels, each
In turn crouched by the other's gnarled feet
Gripping a two-edged, new blue blade
To pare off hard corns, galls, heel calluses,
Then pry clean cotton under ingrown nails.

If she'd read that, she would have bridled: *"Why*
Expose us in our hard times—poor, vulnerable
To the scorn of all and sundry? Not one word
About our larger, finer houses, separate baths
And bedrooms; no slightest recognition we
Might reach a certain prominence in the town."

Or he: *"Now isn't that romantical!—huddled up*
Like monkeys picking fleas. Why not drag in
False teeth or piles? In time, you learn to care
Who gets that close with a razor. Here:
My podiatrist's card. His nurse there was
An old friend—a real good looker, too."

And whose matter is it to restore, to
Maintain this child's crude icon to a faith
They'd both outgrown? Need binds us,
Worn flesh to worn flesh. Abundance reprieves
Us to the self's apostacy, self's accomplishment,
The self's ascendency. Get used to it.

Sitting Outside

These lawn chairs and the chaise lounge
of bulky redwood were purchased for my father
twenty years ago, then plumped down in the yard
where he seldom went while he could still work
and never had stayed long. His left arm
in a sling, then lopped off, he smoked there or slept
while the weather lasted, watched what cars passed,
read stock reports, counted pills,
then dozed again. I didn't go there
in those last weeks, sick of the delusions
they still maintained, their talk of plans
for some boat tour or a trip to the Bahamas
once he'd recovered. Under our willows,
this old set's done well: we've sat with company,
read or taken notes—although the arm rests
dry out and get splintery or wheels drop off
so the whole frame's weakened if it's hauled
across rough ground. Of course the trees, too,
may be less than everlasting: leaves storm down,
branches crack off, the riddled bark
separates, then gets shed. I have a son, myself,
with things to be looked after. I sometimes think
since I've retired, sitting in the shade here
and feeling the winds shift, I must have been filled
with a child's dread you could catch somebody's dying
if you got too close. And you can't be too sure.

Pacemaker

i.

"One Snodgrass, two Snodgrass, three Snodgrass, four . . ."
    I took my own rollcall when I counted seconds;
"One two three, Two two three, Three . . . ," the drum score
    Showed only long rests to the tympani's entrance.

"Oh-oh-oh leff; leff; left-oh-right-oh-leff,"
    The sergeant cadenced us footsore recruits;
The heart, poor drummer, gone lame, deaf,
    Then AWOL, gets frogmarched to the noose.

ii.

Old coots, at the Veterans', might catch breath
    If their cheeks were slapped by a nurse's aide,
Then come back to life; just so, at their birth,
    Young rumps had been tendered warm accolades.

The kick-ass rude attitude, smart-assed insult,
    The acid-fueled book review just might shock
Us back to the brawl like smelling salts,
    Might sting the lulled heart up off its blocks.

iii.

I thought I'd always choose a rubato
    Or syncopation, scorning a fixed rhythm;
        Thought my old heartthrobs could stand up to stress;
Believed one's bloodpump should skip a few beats
    If it fell into company with sleek young women;
        Believed my own *bruit* could beat with the best.

Wrong again, Snodgrass! This new gold gadget
    Snug as the watch on my wife's warm wrist,
        Drives my pulsetempo near twice its old pace—
Go, nonstop startwatch! Go, clockwork rabbit,
    Keep this old lame dog synchronized,
        Steady, sparked up, still in the race.

Packing Up the Lute

I ease you down, your strings set loose
    A tone or three, all twinkle gone,
Into this snug case shaped like a goose
    Or casket for some crook-necked swan,

Your body wrapped in satin cloth,
    Head nestled between blocks of foam,
Lid latched against woodworm and moth
    Then stacked in our attic catacomb

While I—who used to warm and tease you
    Thumbing your belly's deepest cords—
Keep wondering, couldn't we deep-freeze you
    Or lift you on some rocket towards

The icy waste space beyond Mars
    Unfingered by Earth's atmosphere
To shine out with the clear-cut stars
    In some show-stopper of the spheres.

Just keep cool, love; no fault of yours
    Consigns us to this long exile;
Medical science may yet find cures
    For age and carpal tunnel. Meanwhile,

There's not too much left up this sleeve.
    I growl like Melchior, lingering
On stage to ask: "When's the next swan leave?"
    And what's left now I could still sing?

Go lie with lovenotes and snapshots. You
    Were just too fine a vice to last.
Condemned to virtue, we thumb through
    Evidences of our misspent past.

For Hugues Cuenod

—*in his 100th year.*

Midway along our road sometimes a voice
Sounds, prohibiting all heldenblustering choices
    Of timbre, overtones and fashions;
Some fifty years back, I first heard you sing
And thought: "The poems I've been writing lack nothing
    Except such clarity, such passion."

When young, with Nadia Boulanger, you went
Touring through languages and continents,
    Collegia, festivals and venues;
To countertenor from youth's baritone,
You made each form, period and style your own,
    Tasting your way down music's menu.

From Frescobaldi, Couperin, Monteverdi,
To Neidhardt, Bach, Schutz' Sacred Concerti,
    Then Fauré, Debussy and Auric;
From Lassus to "A Lover and His Lass,"
Josquin to Stravinsky's *Rake's Progress*,
    Machaut's Mass to Coward's *Bitter Sweet*.

With an untroubled, easy grace and verve,
You'd fill in for a friend whose wrenched-up nerves
    Failed, sang through 60 years unchanged
By travel, time or untold cigarettes.
At 85, you called your debut at the Met
    "A little bonbon after lunch."

"How could I lose my voice," you were known to banter;
"I never had one"—just a dry, white, unmannered
    Mask tone with the bel canto breathing

That carried your song's deep impulse truly
From mouth to nerve ends like a fine, rich Pouilly.
Why not just say: one voice for all seasons.

Warning

*—on rumors that Richard Wilbur has had a hip
replacement so he could go on playing tennis.*

Hope not that Wilbur's steely hip
Might weaken his ground strokes or grip;
That to shave points or to save sweat
He'd play one game without the net,
Defying the precept that defines
Man's clay court: laying down firm lines.

Our old eyes, cataracted, cleanse
Their vision with a plastic lens;
Clogged arteries flow where we engraft
Teflon with liberating craft
While once-arrested hearts beat time
To Nature's urgent pulse and chime
As pacemakers recoup their prime.

Wilbur's ball and ceramic socket
Propel him like a racing sprocket
To where his artful serve and volley
Dole out love games and melancholy.
Tremble, opponents: learn by this
What power's secured through artifice.

A Forty Gun Salute

—*for Keith and Rosmarie Waldrop on the 40th anniversary
of the Burning Deck Press.*

Cut engines, lights out, silent as the Argo,
A ship glides to some midnight berth beneath
The stern eye of a figure we'll call Waldrop;
Then its co-captains, Rosmarie and Keith,
Unpack it like a trunk from Wells & Fargo:
Layers of illicit lyric that bequeath
Both verse and contraverse, a bootlegged cargo
Of secret moonshine. Sailing in the teeth
Of critics' head winds and the brain's embargo,
Their only life preserver's been a laurel wreath.

Lookouts, if pickled, hoist a bottle's neck
Up to their scopeless eye or down their throat;
Our skippers, daily, made a sober check
Of map, starchart and compass, took due note
Where loose planks could be letting in a small drop
Or so, manned pumps, then veered their Muse's boat
Past rocks, ruins, and many a famous wreck.
All hands, aloft now! Bosuns, pipe this note:
They've kept our old rust-bucket, Burning Deck,
Through 40 storm-torn years, still working, still afloat.

Critic

Anticipate no consequence,
No help, no harm, from Bile's review:
He's never claimed you two are friends
So he'll not quite disembowel you;
Since you're unfashionable these days, you
Can quit worrying he might praise you.

Guru

All hail our hero, Captain Crudd,
That ironclad soul of sperm and blood
Whose cry rang out above the Flood
Calling each man to pull his oar;
Not quite like Captain Bligh, though—more
Like piloting a jug toward shore,
The reasoning of Pooh Bear or
    The voice of Elmer Fudd.

Lifelong

—for the marriage of Charles and Lucina, Candelaria Day,
Feb. 2, 1995. Terminally ill, Charles died Dec. 31, 1996.

So long as you both shall lift
    An echo in night's tunnel, lift
    A child from numbing pavements, lift
    A hand to hold back, to set loose, to enfold;

So long as you both shall leave
    Proud pursuits go their own gait, leave
    The trampling and bright trophies, leave
    Your tidemark on the mind's strand;

So long as you both shall laugh
    At sworn lies and their catch tunes, laugh
    At all contrived, all forced growths, laugh
    From the peaks of occult, calm passion;

So long as you both shall leaf
    Through sanctimonious parchments, leaf
    Gold on a new daybook's edges, leaf
    Out, then blossom the nerves' branchings;

So long as you both shall listen
    To the song latched in the ribs' cage, listen
    To breath, soft, in the next room, listen
    To surfsound down the blood's ways;

So long as you both shall love,
    So long last; none lasts longer.

A Separation Anthem

You can claim you've downsized, pink-slipped
each other, trimmed back to fighting weight.
It's no less a catastrophe and nothing in the world
will teach you otherwise. Or so much. All crises
are midlife crises that restore you to your teens, though
you're rheumatic, rebellious, at loose ends. You still
could sit beside each other at diplomatic dinners
only if you came in on others' arms. The sentence
smoking on your wall means just what
all graffiti mean: your favorite theories
have just disproven and revoked themselves.
Whatever you've learned from each other
must be turned from, turned against—
against each other in the new curriculum.
Whose pillowtalk, now, will substantiate the day done,
the day that's still to do? Love's born-agains,
you're on the lookout for a new salvation.
With the best luck and happy hunting, it's no less
a catastrophe—one that may not kill you
and we wish you every wonder of it.

A Presence

—*Dostoievsky's older brother sometimes made him stand in*
a corner, telling him, "And don't think about a white bear!"

You are the white bear I try
   not to think about, the file
untitled in my computer's cache:
   you are the one piece of a puzzle
already burned, the rhyme no
   sentence of mine ever leads to.

You are the erasure leaving
   an impression, blank, on each page
of my pad, phone number with no
   name, connection that can't find
its voice, the carryover never
   cancelled, not to be restored.

You are the amputee's ghost
   pain, the debt redoubled on
full payment, the dissolving
   membrane whose unfriendly floaters
blur my lens, the emperor's new
   son and heir, the lost white bear.

For the Third Marriage of My First Ex-Wife

i.

Each other's virgin, equally
too virtuous far too long to be
much good to anyone in bed,
much less in their gestalt—who said
you can't be a virgin more than once?
Kept callow, backward on all fronts,
naive as know-nothing tribes that can't
guess how they keep on getting pregnant—
not once in twelve years had we laid
each other right. What we *had* made
were two nerve-wracked, unreconciled,
spoiled children parenting a child.

ii.

The world lay all before us, where
fine ideals and devil-may-care
low lusts entangle in the heat
and dirty virtues of the street.
Some grade-school children nowadays
can tell you more about the ways
of all flesh than those adults who taught
us sexual conduct. Or did not,
blinking at facts that might assuage
love's tensions well before our age
with its synthetic lubricants,
Viagra and penile implants.

iii.

Our daughter, still recovering from
her own divorce, but who's become
a father, in her call at least
as an Episcopalian priest,
will fly down there to officiate
in linking you to your third mate;
only some twenty years ago
that daughter married me also
to the last of my four wives.
This spinoff of our unspent lives
still joins us (though to others) saying: clamp fast
to what's worth holding. Also, save the best for last.

Phone Message

—for that Lady gone on a visit.

In shop for repairs, our hi-fi's gone
Dumbstruck for the third straight month:
Our well-tempered joists and timbers
Forget their known vibrations; our stalled air
Won't admit how well it trembled. That much
You've damped down, three days gone.

Anyone who makes a meal for no one
Except himself will get himself a plate
Full of food. No one dies of that.
Or loses weight. Yet to what purpose
Taste buds? IVs or injections might save
Time. Or eating with just anyone.

Aging, the neurons fail to reach out;
Dendrites tangle and don't end right—
In tight contact with some warm,
Well-lubricated synapse. Names
Won't call up on my screen. Soon now,
Before these Xmas lightstrings blink out,

Throw down the keyhole, Lady; bring back
The dial tone. Let Bach, resounding,
Transfuse the tongue, the appetite, shiver
These timbers, sonar shock on shock;
Defibrillate this whole solar system
If you've a mind to. Why hold back?

The Moth Chorale

In Switzerland, just one half-timbered floor
above sheep flocks and cattles' backs, whole families,
hushed in the updrafts of their warm beasts'
breath and lowing, slept.

Younger, we boogied to the tune of money:
old coin bracelets, clocktock, traintracks, tap-drip,
bottle-rattle from the fridge, our thighs jogging
to our keyring's jingling tango, to the times.

Older, we try to catch the swallows' swoop and glide,
bat-flitter, the courante and gigue of falling water,
sarabande of leaf and leaving, or the limbs' bare
bones, of wake and work, of wane and fallow.

Her den, like Haydn's attic, is at our house's
high far end, her clavichord . . . not that
you actually hear it; you have to read it
the way you'd braille somebody's pulse
through fingers' nerve ends, calculate
the heart's brute *bruit* as that impels
the room's air pressure. I'll go up there
to complain: the Moth Chorale's
been practicing again—crickets, katydids,
ladybugs and lacewings, the ensemble
wingbeat of the world's assembled butterflies;
the timbers of this whole house tremble—
and I'm supposed to concentrate?

Double Forte

In the silent, conditionally holy night,
high shrieks, howls, then wailing wild
chorales of ululation sound the news
that the half-breed coydog pack's
old hunters have come back to their home
kuffuffle, to their own known fracas.

Why, though, so close up near the house?
Still, whyever not? Whenever my wife
drives up from Sunday services where
she's led the hush-voiced choir in psalms,
our housepet—much-trained, well-behaved—
breaks out, all vibrato heldenpoodle.

In Miami, once, two blue-green macaws
at sundown sheered in to their palm's nest
revisiting their family's daybreak wrangle,
while in San Miguel, at sunup, all Venus'
smutty sparrow squadrons squalled
and tumbled through our bougainvillea.

At mid-day makeout matinees, our very own
halloos of joinder and arrival sound out
from the self's high balconies to long-lost
non-Platonic halves. Waking later, shaken,
we fondly hiss: "Assassin! Murdolator! You!"
smirking at what our neighbors must surmise.

Invitation

Come live with me and be my last
Resource, location and resort,
My workday's focus and steadfast
Distraction to a weekend's sport.

Come end up with me, close my list;
Blank my black book, block every e-mail
From ex-loves whose mouths won't be missed;
Let nothing else alive look female.

Come couch with me *mit Freud und Lust*
As every evening's last connection.
Talk to me; prove the day like Proust;
Let what comes next rise to inspection.

Come, let old aftermaths get lost,
Let failures and betrayals mend,
Cancel repayments; clear the cost;
Once more unto the breach, dear friend.

Come lay us down to sleep at least,
Sharing this pillow's picture show.
Who's been my braintrust and best beast?
Who else knows what I need to know?

Afterword

In most cases, these poems are given in chronological order of composition. Considerations of space, however, forbid the inclusion of all parts of short cycles such as *In Flower* or the poems for each season; those parts included here, however, keep their original numbering in small Roman numerals. In a few cases, a poem written for cycles that had already appeared in book form has been included with the earlier cycle.

The poems included here under the heading *Kinder Capers* were written for collaborations with the painter DeLoss McGraw. Since it is impossible to reproduce here the paintings, I have tried to choose the poems best suited to stand alone without the paintings. *Make-Believes*, a volume containing three of our joint projects, giving both poems and color reproductions of McGraw's paintings, has been published by Eatonbrook Editions.

Notes

"Van Gogh: The Starry Night": This poem contains many quotes from Van Gogh's letters (given in italics) and ends with his last words which could mean, "This is the way to go," "I'd like to die like this," or "I want to go home."

"Henrich Himmler, 1 April 1945": This poem contains many quotations from an early manual of astrology.

"Adolf Hitler, 1 April 1945": Passages in quotation marks were actually spoken by Hitler.

"Adolf Hitler, 20 April 1945": Passages in Old German Script are quotations from *Lohengrin*.

"Adolf Hitler, 30 April 1945": Passages in quotation marks were actually spoken by Hitler or written in his diary; passages in Old German Script are quotations from Wagner.

"The Discreet Advantages of a Reichstag Fire": The frenzied response to the burning of the Reichstag (German parliament) Building permitted the Nazi government to become an absolute tyranny.

"On the Streets": The Spanish line means "I don't have any change."

"Song Slam": All italicized lines come from songs about song and singing.

"At Home, Lost": The italicized line is a Greek emperor's decree on a captured Bulgarian army.

"Chasing Fireflies": based in part on a painting by DeLoss McGraw. Cf. also Andrew Marvell, "The Mower to the Glowworms," ll. 1–2:

> Ye living lamps, by whose dear light
> The nightingale does sit so late

and "Damon the Mower," ll. 41–42:

> I am the Mower Damon, known
> By all the meadows I have mown.

"Packing Up the Lute": Lauritz Melchior, singing *Lohengrin* one night at the Met, reportedly asked the question given in quotations when the swan-boat which was to take him back to the Other World passed him by and disappeared into the stage's wings.

Acknowledgments

The author is deeply grateful for a period spent in residence at the Rockefeller Foundation's Villa Serbeloni in Bellagio, Italy, where a number of these poems were composed.

Grateful acknowledgment is made to the editors and publishers of publications in which poems (or earlier versions) of the "New Poems" section appeared:

Agenda (England): "Packing Up the Lute," "A Presence," "Nocturnes ii–vii," and "Lifelong";

American Poetry Review: "Farm Kids," "Leavings," "On High," "Sitting Outside," "A Separation Anthem," and "Invitation";

Atlantic Monthly: "Fast Foods: A Rap Rondeau";

Cincinnati Review: "Seasoned Chairs for a Child";

Early Music America: "For Hugues Cuenod in his 100th Year";

The Formalist: "Warning," "A Forty Gun Salute," and "Critic";

Harvard Review: "Song Slam," "Lady!—," and "Daylilies";

The New Criterion: "Packing Up the Lute";

The New York Quarterly: "Ruffed Grouse," and "Guru";

Ploughshares: "Night Voices";

Poetry: "Who Steals My Good Name," "Nightwatchman's Song," "Pacemaker," and "For the Third Marriage of My First Ex-Wife";

The Post Standard, Syracuse, NY: "Talking Heads";

Rosebud: "Warning";

Southern Review: "Parents," "Lasting," "At the Villa," "Double Forte" (there titled "Fortement"), "Phone Message," "On the Streets," and "The Moth Chorale";

Spread (Democracy Issue): "Chasing Fireflies";

Van Gogh's Ear (France): "Gringolandia."

About the Author

W. D. Snodgrass was born in Beaver Falls, Pennsylvania, in 1926. He served in the U.S. Navy during World War II and later took a BA, MA and MFA from the State University of Iowa. After graduating, he taught at various universities, among them Wayne State, Delaware, and Syracuse. His first book of poems, *Heart's Needle*, received the Pulitzer Prize in 1960, and he has received numerous awards and honors for his poetry, translations, and criticism. He and his wife, Kathleen, divide their time between Erieville, New York, and San Miguel de Allende, Mexico.

BOA Editions, Ltd., American Poets Continuum Series

Colophon

Not for Specialists: New and Selected Poems by W. D. Snodgrass
is set in Monotype Dante with text design
by Richard Foerster, York Beach, Maine.
The cover design is by Daphne Poulin-Stofer.
The cover art, "W. D. Under Arrest" by DeLoss McGraw,
is courtesy of the author & the artist.
Manufacturing is by McNaughton & Gunn, Lithographers,
Saline Michigan.

→><←

The publication of this book is made possible, in part,
by the special support of the following individuals:

Alan & Nancy Cameros
Gwen & Gary Conners
Wyn Cooper & Shawna Parker
Susan DeWitt Davie
Dorothea Diver & Barton Sutter
Peter & Suzanne Durant   →><←   Suressa & Dick Forbes
Bev & Pete French
Susan Goodman & Carl Dawson
Dane & Judy Gordon
Kip & Deb Hale
Peter & Robin Hursh
Robert & Willy Hursh
X. J. Kennedy   →><←   Archie & Pat Kutz
Rosemary & Lew Lloyd
John & Barbara Lovenheim
Art Lyons   →><←   Ruth & Irving Malin
Peter & Phyllis Makuck
Jimmy & Wendy Mnookin
Marianne & David Oliveiri
Boo Poulin   →><←   Dona Rosu   →><←   Thomas R. Ward
Pat & Michael Wilder
Glenn & Helen William